HIDDEN
GARDENS *of* PARIS

HIDDEN GARDENS *of* PARIS

A Guide to the Parks, Squares, and Woodlands of the City of Light

SUSAN CAHILL

PHOTOGRAPHS BY MARION RANOUX

ST. MARTIN'S GRIFFIN ❧ NEW YORK

www.stmartins.com

Map by Joseph Cahill

Design by Fritz Metsch

Library of Congress Cataloging-in-Publication Data

Cahill, Susan Neunzig.
   Hidden gardens of Paris : a guide to the parks, squares, and woodlands of the City of Light / Susan Cahill ; photographs by Marion Ranoux.—1st ed.
       p. cm.
Includes bibliographical references.
  ISBN 978-0-312-67333-8 (trade pbk.)
  ISBN 978-1-4668-0216-2 (e-book)
  1. Gardens—France—Paris. 2. Gardens—France—Paris—Pictorial works. I. Ranoux, Marion. II. Title.
  SB466.F82P3724 2012
  635.0944′361—dc23

2011043824

First Edition: April 2012

10 9 8 7 6 5 4 3 2

For Nina,
enfant de Paris,
enfant de mon coeur

CONTENTS

AROUND BASTILLE AND NORTHEASTERN PARIS

INTRODUCTION

Look inside the green heart of Paris and you will see the exquisite beauty of one of the world's most cherished places. That beauty quickens the love of life and stirs our desire for more. People—travelers—always want to come back to Paris again and again. This book guides us to forty of its loveliest pleasures, the small squares and gardens, the thrilling open spaces bordered by architectural elegance, the parks and sprawling woodlands of Europe's crown jewel, Paris, the City of Light. This book also searches the legacy of each space, the fertile culture of art or history or character that lives in the consciousness of the city.

Paris is more and more a green city. The current mayor has added more than one hundred new acres to its four hundred existing green spaces. To protect them, the city has re-choreographed the flow of traffic; bicycles have been restored to their once major role; pedestrians own more of the streets. Mayor Delanoe's commitment to an environmentally healthy city has made environmentally friendly travel a real possibility for the millions of visitors whom Paris welcomes every year.

Such travel is wonderfully stress-free, cutting down on the hassles that can turn a beautiful place into tourist hell—crowded stuffy museums and shops, long lines, packed bistros, tourists' cameras, the fatigue of not being able to sit down. Green Paris is the alternative to this hell. Some gardens have even been described as "paradisial."

There's the balm of tall old trees, bright flower gardens, fountains, and ponds delicious to the singing birds. On the surrounding benches and chairs, under what Colette calls "the great ceiling of the Parisian sky," people are reading *Le Monde*, enjoying the sun and the soft-spoken company of one another. The quiet can be seductive, opening your mind to ruminations that fast-paced travel does not have time for, questions about where you are and why you came. In the Middle Ages, the garden attached to the cloister—*hortus conclusus*—was a haven for the soul, a private sanctuary. Sitting and gazing and smelling the jasmine in any Paris green space, you have time to wonder if it's true that, for instance, "Paris is the abode of love, as well as of violence," that despite the dark side, "which is only sometimes . . . love is there all the time, in a cat arching its back in the sun, and in the eyes of *la belle boulangère* in her white apron."* Sitting in *Square Boucicaut* or lying on the grass in *Parc Bercy* where the children's carousel plays the Bach Brandenburgs, there's time and space to think.

Some havens are famous and easy to find. Others are off the beaten track, tucked away. Without a guide—*Hidden Gardens of Paris*—they're easy to miss. The idyllic *Vallée Suisse*, for example—*Swiss Valley*—is invisible from the street, accessible only if you know how to find the path that leads down to the little waterfall and pond, the lilacs under beech trees—the surprise of this unexpected peace and solitude in the middle of a big, noisy city. As I think back on the *Vallée Suisse* (or any number of the places listed in this book's Contents), theories about the healing power of gardens ring true:

*Richard Cobb, *Paris and Elsewhere*.

The garden . . . seeks to be different from the ordinary world, offering the possibility of heightened experience— spiritual, sensuous, or both—through communion with things of the earth. A rock, a tree, a well of light invites our attention to sun and sky, wind and water, trees, plants, flowers, birds and secret animals, insects, bugs, soil, all set apart from the larger world. In that sense the garden is a "sacred space."*

The best way to get to know green Paris is to walk, discovering as you move from one *arrondissement* to another the jumble of neighborhoods, or *quartiers*, and identities that only pedestrians have a chance to find. Julia Child writes about learning the city on her own two feet, walking everywhere (including the out-of-the-way *Parc des Buttes-Chaumont*).[†] And though the indefatigable Julia doesn't mention it, the métro provides efficient service in getting you to a particular *quartier*. But once you hit the streets, you need only the *Hidden Gardens of Paris*, a good map, and your two feet. Walking is itself a kind of enlightenment: *solvitur ambulando*—"It is solved by walking"—as they said in the Middle Ages. You come to understand what those who do not move beyond the posh city center cannot: Paris is ordinary, scruffy, individualistic, bizarre, broken, endlessly inventive, secretive, tender, haunted with history, generous with pretty squares away from the boulevards.

The beautiful photographs accompanying the commentary about each of the oases show these multiple personalities. They show, too, a range of landscape styles, from the classically

---

* Catherine Howett, *The Meaning of Gardens.*
† Julia Child, *My Life in France.*

formal to the romantically ungroomed. In these images, the beauty of Paris becomes even more seductive: the photographs capture the real city, having perspectives that go beyond the famous center to the less visited *quartiers* of the northwest, the northeast, and the east: Verlaine's *Square des Batignolles,* for instance, or the charming *Promenade Plantée.*

My commentary about the legacy of each place sketches an aspect of its cultural significance layered within the colorful history of Paris. Many Parisian places have been called "sites of memory," where "the historical consciousness of the French people has focused."* Over time these places become repositories of the city's collective memory. The storied view of the vast *Bois de Boulogne,* for example, is as the setting of secret love and illicit sex. But the spaces of green Paris also comprise multiple and conflicting memories: of great characters and geniuses (Colette in the *Palais-Royal;* Chopin and George Sand, lovers, then enemies, in their respective gardens); of the making of art and beauty (the gardens of Delacroix, Balzac, Rodin); of violent historical events (the Saint Bartholomew's Day Massacre in the lovely *Tuileries,* the Siege of Paris and the Paris Commune on the gorgeous *Montmartre butte,* the German Occupation in the pretty *Luxembourg*). Paris does not forget. But these sites of historical violence appear today, simultaneously, as havens of consoling beauty.

Each of the forty commentaries is followed by a listing of nearby places that are part of the cultural richness—the lasting greenness—of a site or neighborhood. A few good cafés, bistros, and bars are also listed, as well as bookstores. Paris is, well, fertile, with books, book buyers, and park-

*Colin Jones, *Paris: The Biography of a City.*

bench readers. Many of the titles included in the footnotes were recommended by Paris booksellers, who, to a woman, to a man, are savvy readers themselves. For travelers, and in particular for armchair travelers, the Sources provide wide and deep angles on the City of Light.

Coming to feel at home in the outdoors of this living, breathing city—getting to know the hidden gardens of Paris— you'll find there are many ways to smell the roses, the sweetness of the world you've walked your way into, beautiful in the vastness of memory.

ÎLE DE LA CITÉ

Square du Vert Galant behind the Pont Neuf

SQUARE DU VERT GALANT

ENTRANCE: from the Pont Neuf, descend the staircase
   behind the statue of Henri IV
MÉTRO: Pont Neuf
HOURS: 9–dark

Astride the Pont Neuf, Henri IV seems to welcome us to the *Île de la Cité,* "the head, the heart, the very marrow of the whole city."* The leafy green triangular square behind the bridge is named for that lusty gallant on horseback who loved his city mightily, especially its wine, women, and good times. Once you descend the staircase and enter the square, *Vert Galant* presents a magical combination of delights: a strong, wide river, flowers and grass, a riverbank shaded with willows and a prospect of magnificent architecture: the Louvre on the right and the gold-domed Institut de France on the left. There's also, in early evening in all seasons, a fair portion of privacy, a promise of intimacy.

This romantic western tip of the boat-shaped *Île de la Cité*—the original settlement of the Parisii, a Celtic tribe subdued by Caesar—is a fitting introduction to the City of Light. For from the beginning, Paris has been an object of affection: (the Romans called it *Lutetia*)—*Cara Lutetia,* "my beloved Lutetia," in the words of the late Roman emperor Julian in 358 AD.† As king, *le Vert Galant Henri IV*

*Guy de Bazoches, "Description de Paris vers 1175."
†Colin Jones, *Paris: The Biography of a City.*

(1589–1610) declared his intention "to make this city beautiful, tranquil, . . . desiring to make a whole world of this city and a wonder of the world."* Such triumphs as the elegant *Pont Neuf* (the "new bridge" is the oldest bridge in Paris), the *Place Dauphine* opposite the bridge, and the *Place Royale* (later renamed *Place des Vosges*) show his genius as architect and urban visionary. His energetic love life—he had two wives, at least fifty-six mistresses, and households full of bastards—also won him the heart of Parisians (until his serial amours began to bore and irritate).

But Henri the obsessive lover was above all a peacemaker. Born and raised a Protestant by a rigidly reformist mother, he converted to Catholicism, the religion of the majority, to end the long religious wars between Catholics and Protestants that by the end of the sixteenth century had left Paris starving and looking like a bomb site. Detesting religious partisanship, he drafted and signed the Edict of Nantes (1598), which put toleration of the religion he had renounced on the books. Sounding like a Dalai Lama, he explained:

> *Those who honestly follow their conscience are of my religion, and as for me, I belong to the faith of all those who are gallant and good. . . . We must be brought to agreement by reason and kindness and not by strictness and cruelty which serve only to arouse men.*

The fanatical Catholic who stabbed him to death, François Ravaillac, was not persuaded.

But to this day, in the words of André Maurois, "together

* Jean-Pierre Babelon, "Henri IV, urbaniste de Paris," in *Festival du Marais*, 1966.

with Charlemagne, Joan of Arc, and Saint-Louis IX, Henri IV remains one of France's heroes." He declared kindness and mercy the primary virtues of a prince.*

Nearby

PLACE DAUPHINE *Enter through rue Henri Robert on the east side of Pont Neuf. Henri IV designed this hideaway for his son Louis XIII—the dauphin—who was nine years old when his father was assassinated. Some of the low brick buildings are of Henri's period; the trees are new and small, having only recently been planted to replace the white chestnuts that were attacked by a virulent pest. Yves Montand and Simone Signoret, who loved the village-like Place, lived here.*

PONT DES ARTS *The footbridge connecting the Left Bank to the Louvre carries a lively traffic of musicians, painters, students, lovers, tourists, and children, with a wide view of the Seine and a rear view of the* **Square du Vert Galant.** *Pierre Auguste Renoir's painting* Le Pont des Arts *(1868) was the first he sold to the art dealer Paul Durand-Ruel, one of the most important advocates for French impressionists in Europe and the United States.*

SQUARE HONORÉ-CHAMPION *Through an arch to the right of the* **Institut de France** *on the Left Bank's Quai de Conti, a statue of the eighteenth-century philosopher* **Voltaire** *stands atop a small green mound bordered with flowers. Without this immensely influential leader of the Enlightenment, the Declaration of Independence (and the American Revolution) would*

---

* André Maurois, *A History of France*.

never, according to Benjamin Franklin and Thomas Jefferson, have come to pass.

LES BOUQUINISTES *The quintessentially Parisian version of bookselling. The large green standing boxes full of books and prints line the quais on both banks of the Seine. The first ones were located on* **Pont Neuf.**

Square Jean-XXIII and the Cathedral Gardens of Notre-Dame of Paris

SQUARE JEAN-XXIII

ENTRANCE: the riverside and east end of the Cathedral of Notre-Dame of Paris

MÉTRO: Cité

HOURS: 8—8:30

Until 1831, when it was destroyed in a riot, the palace of the archbishop of Paris occupied the land between *Notre-Dame* and the Seine. Both the palace gardens and the cathedral had long been revered sites in this *quartier* of religious associations dating back to the fourth century when Emperor Julian presided in a temple dedicated to Jupiter. These Roman ruins became the foundation of the basilica of *Saint-Étienne* (Saint Stephen) in 528 and the first Notre-Dame. The new Notre-Dame, begun in 1163, stands today, after centuries of renovations and the fanatical rampages of the Terror, as one of the crown jewels of Gothic architecture not only in Paris but all over Europe.

The new cathedral gardens are dedicated to the memory of Pope John XXIII, born Angelo Roncalli (1881–1963), in Lombardy, the papal nuncio in Paris from 1944 to 1953 who went on to become the "good pope" and the progenitor of the Second Vatican Council (1962–1965). "Jesus came to break down the barriers," he preached. "The central point of his teaching is love." Parisians remember Roncalli's long walks through the city accompanied by his friends, Protestants, Catholics, Jews, agnostics, atheists. At diplomatic receptions he enjoyed the champagne and the conviviality of men and women. He read French literature and knew the post–World War II French intellectuals and theologians, whom he would invite to participate in the reforms of Vatican II. A savvy diplomat, he was trusted by the French government. On the occasion of being awarded the Legion of Honor, President Auriol praised him for understanding and respecting "the traditions of justice and tolerance," the honor of the French nation.

Flowering cherry trees, in luxuriant bloom along the south porches in April, screen but do not hide the original medallions that bear images of student life. Beds of daffodils and tulips run the length of the cathedral's southern flank as far as the eastern end, where flying buttresses rise above a small square generous with flowers, benches, and travelers taking their ease. The mood here often feels more peaceful than *Notre-Dame*'s interior, where getting stuck behind a crush of tourists aiming cameras at the stained glass is almost inevitable. Lambert Strether, however, the protagonist of Henry James's *The Ambassadors,* notes the "beneficent action on his nerves" of sitting alone "in the great dim church," soothed in this "place of refuge," with "a sense of safety, of simplification."

The inviting square beneath the flying buttresses is a fitting memorial to the genial man who confessed a deep sadness when he was recalled from Paris to Rome: "I love France and I love Paris," he told a friend, "and I hoped to stay a little longer. I can't really see myself in Rome."*

---

* Thomas Cahill, *Pope John XXIII.*

Nearby

GARDEN OF THE HÔTEL-DIEU   *On the left of the plaza as you face the western front of* **Notre-Dame**. *Founded in 651 by Bishop Saint-Landry,* **Hôtel-Dieu** *(since rebuilt) is the oldest public hospital in Paris. Leave behind the hordes queuing for Notre-Dame, enter the lobby, and bear right, then left, into the lower garden. Go up the stairs to the larger upper garden, where you will find flowers and calm and a place to sit.*

LA MÉMORIAL DES MARTYRS DE LA DÉPORTATION   *Off Square de l'Île de France, the eastern tip of Île de la Cité. Cross Quai Archévêque and enter the small rose garden (weekends, 8–9; weekdays, 7:30) surrounded by the Seine and facing Île Saint-Louis. Beneath the garden, down a narrow staircase, the writings on the walls of the memorial to the French martyrs of the Nazi Deportation are by Eluard, Saint-Exupéry, Sartre, Aragon, Desnos. Tues–Sun, 10–12; 2–7.*

THE LEFT BANK

View of Notre-Dame from Square René-Viviani on the Left Bank

The Latin Quarter

SQUARE RENÉ-VIVIANI

ENTRANCES: 25, quai de Montebello; rue Lagrange;
    rue Saint-Julien le Pauvre
MÉTRO: Maubert-Mutualité; Saint-Michel; Cité
HOURS: Open every day until 9:30

The Gothic glory of *Notre-Dame de Paris* presents a dramatic angle to this small Left Bank square along the Seine. Any weekday around noon, a few Parisians sit under the trees, reading, painting watercolors; children chase pigeons, a tourist eats a salad. There's a tall bronze fountain in the center (by Georges Jeanclos, 1995) that tells the story of *Saint-Julien le Pauvre*, the name of the small church in the square's southwest corner, perhaps the oldest in the city. (It was built in 1170–1240 on the ruins of the sixth-century church of Saint-Julien the Martyr.)

Up close on the fountain you see sculpted images, motifs of the medieval legend about Saint-Julien: a stag, drops of tears, a river, a forest, as well as words from the adaptation by Gustave Flaubert, "The Legend of Saint Julien," in his *Three Tales* (1876). A traveler made curious by the fountain's inscription could pick up a copy of the Flaubert collection in the nearby bookstore *Shakespeare and Company,* a few minutes' walk to the west on *rue de la Bûcherie,* and then follow Flaubert's retelling while studying the images and words on the fountain. It's a religious story, unusual for Flaubert, appropriate to the place where the ancient church and the new fountain remember it: Julien, a "savage heart," possessed of a blood

thirst similar to a wild animal's, murders his parents. He re-
pents, lives alone in the wild, becoming a poor Hospitaller
who devotes himself to helping lepers and ferrying them
and other poor travelers across a river. At the end, there is a
mystical and tender scene of transformation, such as never
lightened the conclusion of *Madame Bovary*: a leper, who is
Christ himself, embraces Julien and, in Flaubert's words, "the
firmament unfolded—and Julian rose up into the blue of
space, face to face with Our Lord Jesus, who bore him off to
heaven." The decorations on the fountain evoke a tradition
of *tendresse* and compassion that **Square René-Viviani** commemorates. An annex of the **Hôtel-Dieu,** the public hospital
for the poor, once stood here. And the square is named for the
politician who, with Jean Jaurès and Nobel Peace Prize winner Aristide Briand, founded the Socialist Party of France,
originally intended to provide a network of helping services
for workers and for people who had nothing.

The square sinks into deep shade on its south side, benches
under trees offering a place to sit out of the sun. What is said
to be the oldest tree in Paris, a *Robinia* (an acacia), planted in
1601 by Jean Robin, botanist and director of the royal apoth-
ecary garden, stands along the path to the ancient church,
which hosts concerts.

Nearby

SHAKESPEARE AND COMPANY   *37, rue de la Bûcherie. A
scruffy English-language bookshop packed from floor to ceiling
with new and used books, the descendant of the original shop in
rue de l'Odéon where owner and publisher Sylvia Beach published
James Joyce's* Ulysses *in 1922. A fun place on Bloomsday, June*

16, with readings and wine-tasting upstairs. There's a good selection of books about Paris on the right wall as you enter.

GARDEN OF THE CHURCH OF SAINT-SÉVERIN *A short walk west, across rue Saint-Jacques, to the rear entrance of the church. A series of engravings by Georges Roualt*—**Miserere**—*hangs in the oval-shaped chapel of the Holy Sacrament. The garden can only be entered from inside the church (begun in the thirteenth century, to accommodate the students from the Sorbonne) through a doorway in the fourth bay on the south wall; it's surrounded by the city's only surviving charnel house, the repository for bones dug up from a burial ground when it became full.*

ABBEY BOOKSHOP *A block south of the church at 29,* **rue de la Parcheminerie** *(named for the bookbinders and illustrators who worked in this street from the twelfth century), the shop has a huge selection of new and secondhand books and a bookseller who can put his hands on whatever title you request before you blink. Ask for Brian Spence, the helpful owner, who also guides weekend tours into the countryside. Mon–Sat 10–7. www.abbeybookshop.net.*

Gardens of the Musée de Cluny

JARDINS DU MUSÉE DE CLUNY

ENTRANCE: corner of boulevard Saint-Michel and
     boulevard Saint-Germain-des-Prés
MÉTRO:Saint-Michel
HOURS: daily, 9:15–5:45

These small enclosed gardens feel undiscovered and private, the traffic beyond the boulevard's high hedges just a murmur. Inspired by medieval models, they are arranged thematically. "The Love Garden," in season fragrant with roses, symbolizes the object of the heart's desire: "The rose is Beauty and Love." In the Middle Ages it was Mary's flower, the central stained-glass image on the façade of Notre-Dame, Chartres, and other Gothic cathedrals.* Plantings of hazel, elder, quince, and holly fill "The Forest of the Unicorn." "The Children's Glade" imitates a medieval bestiary: rabbits, foxes, and a unicorn play and hide. "The Heavenly Garden," beneath the shadows of a stately tree of flamboyantly wide branches, signifies the garden as a figure of the soul, a private sanctuary, attached to the cloister—*hortus conclusus*—an image found in the biblical *Song of Songs* and the writings of medieval women mystics.† The thirteenth-century Hadewijch saw the garden of the *Song of Songs* as an emblem of a mystical relationship between the soul—personified as female—and the God of Love:

*Allan Temko, *Notre-Dame of Paris*.
†Susan Cahill, *Wise Women*.

You ravish my heart, my sister, my promised bride, . . .
How delicious is your love, more delicious than wine!
How fragrant your perfumes, more fragrant than all spices! . . .
She is a garden enclosed, my sister, my promised bride;
a garden enclosed, a sealed fountain.

"The Heavenly Garden" is also a metaphor for the Blessed Virgin Mary, the bride of the *Song of Songs* according to Christian interpretation, her love for humanity manifested in lily of the valley, violets, daisies, roses, and strawberries. As in all monastic cloister gardens, the intimacy between the soul's interiority and a sensory embrace of life is palpable, expressive of a time that "had little difficulty in squaring love of God with love of worldly beauty and of the sensuous world."* In the High Middle Ages and especially in Paris, *amor mundi* was a state of beatitude.

Nearby

THE LADY WITH THE UNICORN TAPESTRIES   *Located in room 13 on the first floor of the Musée du Moyen Age (Hôtel de Cluny); open daily except Tues, 9:15–5:45. The path from the gardens leads around the corner to* **6, place Paul-Painlevé,** *the entrance to the museum. The scarlet red background of the six tapestries, woven in wool and silk in the* mille-fleurs, *or thousand flowers, design, are strewn with tiny flowers, plants, and birds, each one an exquisite garden world of allegorical mystery, beautifully lit and displayed. Five of the tapestries symbolize the five senses. In the fourth, the Lady weaves a wreath of carnations and a monkey inhales the perfume of a rose, evoking the sense of smell.*

* Alistair Horne, *Seven Ages of Paris.*

Following the medieval taste for multiple symbolism, the unicorn can be seen as both a religious and a profane image, both a Christ figure and a lover.

LIBRAIRIE COMPAGNIE *58, rue des Écoles, across from Balzar, next to Square Paul-Painlevé, this* librairie *has a complete inventory of French literature, reviews, and journals.*

MICHEL DE MONTAIGNE *The bronze statue of the great philosopher-essayist (1533–1592) on* rue des Écoles, *on the south side of Square Paul-Painlevé, is a favorite icon of the Latin Quarter, regularly touched and caressed by passing students. "I have seen the leaves, the flowers, and the fruit," he wrote in old age. "Now I see the withering—happily, since it is natural."*

BRASSERIE BALZAR *49, rue des Écoles, diagonally across from Square Paul-Painlevé. A longtime fixture on the itinerary of Left Bank intelligentsia and artists, done up with mirrors, paintings, plants, and windows facing rue des Écoles.*

CHAMPO *The legendary movie theater is located on the corner of rue Champollion at 51, rue des Écoles. Walk up Champollion, past more theaters, to Place de la Sorbonne.*

Square Paul-Langevin, beneath la Montagne Sainte-Geneviève

SQUARE PAUL-LANGEVIN

ENTRANCE: corner of rue Monge and rue des Écoles
MÉTRO: Cardinal Lemoine; Maubert-Mutualité
HOURS: 8–dusk, according to the season

Bordered with flowers into late autumn, this square draws attention to the *Montagne Sainte-Geneviève,* which rises behind it. As a site of memory it bears witness to the Latin Quarter's tradition of intellectual and artistic brilliance that first flourished in the Parisian Middle Ages. It's named for physicist **Paul Langevin** (1872–1946), renowned for his discovery of ultrasound, the process of echolocation, used to detect the presence of German submarines. Acclaimed throughout the European scientific community, Langevin, a fierce opponent of Nazism (whose daughter, *une Résistante*, survived imprisonment in several concentration camps), was removed from his position at the École de Physique et Chimie by the Vichy government. He outlived the Occupation and is buried over the hill in the Panthéon (climb the serpentine *rue de la Montagne Sainte-Geneviève* to the *Place du Panthéon*), the monumental tomb of France's great men and women. Buried near Langevin are the remains of his mentors Pierre and Marie Curie. After Pierre Curie's death, Marie Curie and Langevin had an affair; Langevin was still married and had four children. Marie Curie, who was born in Poland, was ostracized as a foreigner and condemned in the right-wing press—they accused her of being a Jew—and her home was attacked by a mob while she was in Stockholm picking up her second Nobel Prize.

The Square also commemorates, in a statue of *François Villon* (1431–1472), the first modern poet of France as well as the last great poet of the Middle Ages. In a time of violent death, famine, and invasion, Villon lived the lawless life of a perpetual student in the lawless Latin Quarter, this Left Bank student neighborhood where, from the beginning, Latin was the language of the schools. Villon, fighting over a girl, killed a priest in self-defense, thieved, womanized, and was jailed regularly, almost executed, finally exiled.* The songs he wrote are boisterous, the poems lyrical evocations of the era's melancholy and nostalgia for the optimism of the High Middle Ages: the refrain *"Mais où sont les neiges d'antan?"* (Where are the snows of yesteryear?) is from the poem "Ballade des Dames du Temps Jadis" ("The Ballad of the Women of Yore"). The prayers and songs he wrote to Mary—his *"Dame des ciel"* (Lady of heaven)—are as sweetly passionate as his love poems. Published posthumously in Paris in 1489, Villon as poet and bohemian would later appeal to such poets as Verlaine, Pound, and Huysmans.

The south side of the square fits into the high rear wall of what was formerly the *École Polytechnique* (since moved to the suburbs) and is now the Research Ministry. A charming old moss-covered fountain is embedded in the wall, which is covered with ivy and flowers and sculpted angels by Ingres; behind it, a staircase overflowing with viburnum plants looks like a green mossy sculpture. The children's playground, filled with fathers and kids on a Sunday afternoon, is wonderful to

---

* Colin Jones, *Paris: The Biography of a City.*

behold while you sit waiting for the movie to start a few doors west at *Action École Cinéma,* 23, rue des Écoles.

Nearby

L'HARMATTAN   *25, rue des Écoles. An academic bookstore chain; the DVD store stocks classics of French cinema. Helpful service.*

JARDIN CARRÉ   *Enter at 11, rue Descartes, to the left as you ascend from* **rue des Écoles** *(bearing left at the square). A serene and sprawling green space of topiary with a square pool in the center, it's a public hideaway for academic families of the Sorbonne. On the grounds of some of the original fourteenth-century colleges, it was created in the courtyard of the original building of the École Polytechnique (1794). You see its rear ivy-covered wall from* **Square Paul-Langevin.**

MONTAGNE SAINTE-GENEVIÈVE   *Continue up rue Descartes from Jardin Carré, and turn right into rue Clovis, which leads past* **Lycée Henri IV** *to* **Place Sainte-Geneviève.**

The Students' Garden: L'École Normale Supérieure

L'ÉCOLE NORMALE SUPÉRIEURE
(THE STUDENTS' GARDEN)

ENTRANCE: 45, rue d'Ulm
MÉTRO: Censier Daubenton; Place Monge
HOURS: weekdays during school hours; some weekends

The students' garden opens into a circular retreat around a splashing fountain under tall trees, boughs spread wide and low over benches and flower beds. It's an idyllic place, the undertone of conversation, serious and animated, an ongoing background thrum. The branches of a robust holly tree reach toward the sky. Above the graceful windows recessed under the roof of the school's surrounding walls are the stone heads of French genius: Foucault, Aragon, Lavoisier, Descartes, Pascal, Corneille, Molière, Racine, La Fontaine, Bossuet, Voltaire, Rousseau, Chateaubriand—a pantheon of secular gods high in the serious air.

The historian Tony Judt visited here in 1970 when he was an undergraduate at Cambridge. Probing "the mystery of French intellectuality" in his memoir *Paris Was Yesterday*, he asserts that to achieve clarity one must begin here, at the *École Normale*:

> Founded in 1794 to train secondary school teachers, it became the forcing house of the republican elite. Between 1850 and 1970, virtually every Frenchman of intellectual distinction (women were not admitted until recently) graduated from it.*

*Tony Judt, "Historian's Progress," *New York Review of Books*, March 11, 2010.

Sartre, Pasteur, Durkheim, Pompidou, Péguy, Derrida, Bergson, Rolland, Althusser, Debray, Paul Langevin—each man started out as a *normalien*. (Samuel Beckett taught here when he first came to Paris in 1928.) Neither Judt nor the guidebooks mention the brilliant women such as Simone de Beauvoir who passed through the *École Normale* (women were admitted to *ENS* long before Judt's visit, but their campus was separate from rue d'Ulm's; it was eventually joined with it).

One of the most intriguing of the female *normaliens* was the philosopher, political activist, and mystic *Simone Weil* (1909–1943). Though plagued by a feeling of intellectual inferiority throughout her privileged childhood (she would later revile the secular Jewish ethos of her family), Weil achieved academic success at the *École Normale,* graduating *agrége de philosophie*—a degree reserved for the top few graduates. For her moral intensity and activism in leftist causes her fellow students nicknamed her "The Red Virgin" and "The Categorical Imperative in Skirts."* Later on, her writings— the posthumously published *Waiting for God* (1951), *Gravity and Grace* (1947), *The Need for Roots* (1943), and many other volumes—would be important to Albert Camus, who called her "the only great spirit of our time," and to André Gide, who considered her "the best spiritual writer of this century," as well as to Flannery O'Connor, Kenneth Rexroth, Susan Sontag, Anne Carson, Elaine Scarry, and Edward Hirsch. (In his poem "Simone Weil: Lecture on Love," Hirsch emphasizes perhaps her most constant insight: "Affliction is our warrant, the deepest truth / of human existence.") Weil became a believer under the influence of the mystic light of Assisi and the seventeenth-century metaphysical poetry of George

---

*Eric O. Springsted, ed., *Simone Weil.*

Herbert, in particular the poem "Love Bade Me Welcome." A perceptive critic of institutional Christianity, she refused baptism. Earlier she had rejected membership in the French Communist Party, though for many years she thought of herself as a communist. She had no use, she said, for authoritarian organizations that practiced *anathema sit* ("let him be anathema").* In 2009, *La Passion de Simone* by Finnish composer Kaija Saariaho was produced to critical acclaim in Europe and New York, an oratorio based on Weil's difficult ascetic philosophy and her austere, eccentric life (some say she starved herself to death out of sympathy for the poor people of France who were starving under the Nazi Occupation).

Nearby

MONTAGNE SAINTE-GENEVIÈVE *A very ancient quarter. Follow rue d'Ulm north to* **Place du Panthéon,** *then bear right to* **Place Sainte-Geneviève,** *an open space in front of the* **Église Saint-Étienne du Mont.** *Here on the (not very high)* **Montagne** *are the academic institutions—the* **Sorbonne** *and the* **grandes écoles**—*where most of France's political leaders, philosophers, artists, and scientists got their start. (John Calvin and Ignatius Loyola attended at the same time.) The* **Montagne's** *intellectual lineage goes back to Peter Abélard, the famous teacher, philosopher, and lover of Héloise, who in about 1100 moved here to the Left Bank to escape the conservative cathedral school of Notre-Dame on the Île de la Cité. Away from the strictures of the hierarchy, he and his fellow scholars could teach with more independence. The Paris schools, chartered in 1215 as the Université de Paris,*

---

*Simone Pétrement, *Simone Weil: A Life.*

attracted students and hell-raisers such as François Villon from all over Europe. Though much transformed, the **Latin Quarter** *remains the heart of the students' neighborhood, its old cafés (mostly gone) once the hangouts of poets (Baudelaire, Huysmans, Mallarmé, Verlaine) and the insurgents of 1848, 1871, and 1968.*

PLACE DE LA SORBONNE   *The university's busy courtyard, presided over by a statue of* **Auguste Comte** *and a long fountain bordered by lime trees, café terraces, and shops.*

Arènes de Lutèce

SQUARE DES ARÈNES DE LUTÈCE

ENTRANCE: 10, rue des Arènes, Square Capitan
MÉTRO: Place Monge; Jussieu; Cardinal Lemoine
HOURS: winter, 8–5:30; summer, until 10

The *Latin Quarter*'s best-preserved remnant of the Roman occupation, the arena functions now as a public space used by neighborhood residents for ordinary pleasures. There is no trace of the splendid Roman residences or imperial palace from the time when the *Celtic Parisii* were conquered by Caesar. Kids play football, run through the playgrounds; couples sit on the bleachers of the ancient (much restored) Roman theater enjoying the sunset or a long spring afternoon. The hillsides that rise to surround the arena are deep with flowering shrubbery and trees—hemlocks, evergreens, luxuriant holly. The arena is also framed by the façades of tall mansions that arc along the stately uphill curve of *rue de Navarre.* The arena feels sheltered and out of the way, a local enclave that's off the beaten track and likes it that way.

It's built on the ruins of an arena and theater going back to the first century when *Lutetia* was a Roman province, and people, as many as seventeen thousand, sat in these bleachers watching theatrical entertainments, gladiators in combat, and wild animals in circus acts. The male population sat low and close up; the highest seats were reserved for slaves, the poor, and women, as in the Mother City's Colosseum. Two hundred years later, the stones of the amphitheater were taken away to protect the *Île de la Cité* from invading barbarians.

Later the Christians used the space as a burial ground. It took Paris more than sixteen hundred years to investigate what lay buried beneath centuries of rubble and corpses. (Victor Hugo advocated strongly in favor of resurrecting and restoring the architecture of the past.) The dig at *Lutèce* ended in the twentieth century with the final restoration of the unearthed arena as a public park, the accomplishment of archaeologist Joseph-Louis Capitan in 1917–1918; there are green squares named for him on two sides of the arena. The caves from Roman times where the animals were kept and the actors waited for their cues can still be seen at ground level.

Paris has not obsessed about its history as a colony. It forgot or neglected this site for almost two thousand years as if it was just as well to ignore the long and layered memory this place preserves and the fact that from the beginning Parisians have had a taste for bloody public spectacles.

Today the city's Roman past seems remote to the point of unreality as you sit high in the stone bleachers, watching the games of exuberant children, the birds diving in and out of lush greenery, the throbbing concerts and dancing couples on cool summer nights under the stars.

Nearby

CONTRESCARPE AND MOUFFETARD   *Walk west up the slope of rue de Navarre, across rue Monge, and along rue Rollin or rue Lacépède into* **Place de la Contrescarpe**, *a popular and picturesque square lined with plane trees, a favorite of the writers of the 1920s and 1930s. Hemingway remembered* Contrescarpe *(which once stood at the edge of the medieval city) in his short* *story "The Snows of Kilimanjaro" (1938).* Walk south on the ancient* **rue Mouffetard** *through the quartier Mouffetard—la Mouffe—past a good bookshop, a few cafés and* boulangeries, *to the morning market stalls selling fruits and vegetables, and at the end, to the storied old church of* **Saint-Médard** *(Tues–Sun, 8–12:30; 2:30–7:30) and the small square beside it.*

LIBRAIRIE MICHAEL SEKSIK   *18, rue Lacépède. www.librai riemichaelseksik.com. Open 10–7, closed Sun. A good book-and-print shop, with a strong inventory of old (*ancien*) and modern art books. Also near Jardin des Plantes, across rue Cuvier.*

*Ian Littlewood, *Paris: A Literary Companion.*

The Alpine Garden in the Jardin des Plantes

JARDIN DES PLANTES: JARDIN ALPIN
(THE ALPINE GARDEN)

ENTRANCES: corner of rue Geoffroy Saint-Hilaire and
   rue Buffon; rue Cuvier; quai Saint-Bernard
MÉTRO: Gare d'Austerlitz; Jussieu; Place Monge
HOURS: Apr–Aug, 7:30–8; Sept–Mar, 8–dusk

If you enter the *Jardin des Plantes* from Quai Saint-Bernard (or from the direction of the Austerlitz métro), you'll see stretching before you the often-photographed long promenade that cuts between wide lawns and flower beds groomed to perfection. In spring, midway along, you'll pass flowering cherry trees of an almost unreal luxurance. (Behind the cherry trees is a children's carousel as distinctive as a museum treasure.) Elsewhere in season you'll pass through gardens of roses, peonies, iris, and an orchard of laurel near the children's playground.

In contrast to the formality and grand scale of this introduction, you'll find, off to the right and through a tunnel, the entrance to *le Jardin Alpin*—the Alpine Garden—a hideaway of such delicacy and tranquility it's hard to believe such a place could exist in the middle of a great city. Under a gray sky or blue sunlight, you pass over two thousand species of alpine flowers and plants—white, purple, yellow, and pink—from Pakistan, the Himalayas, Nepal, Afghanistan, the Balkans, Mexico, Argentina, North Africa, the Alps, the Pyrenees, Provence. The genius that has created such a flourishing environment for so many tender plants is supremely evident in the beauty of the garden's design. It's a fragrant place, too, with a few wonderful trees and benches in secluded places to allow you to be alone.

From the exit, bearing right, follow the signposted path to the hill leading through a forest of holly trees and evergreens up to the *labyrinth* with a pagoda at the top. On the way you will pass—near the rue Cuvier entrance—a magnificent cedar of Lebanon; an American sequoia; and in the shade of the forest, the sculpture of *Théodore Monod,* a lifetime luminary at the Musée Nationale d'Histoire Naturelle, his face and head expressing the visionary intelligence behind this magnificent preserve of nature's diversity.

The *Grande Galérie de l'Évolution* (open daily except Tues; located near the entrance of rue Buffon and Geoffroy Saint-Hilaire) presents the story of Mother Nature and her offspring with interactive and dramatic power.

Nearby

MOSQUE GARDEN AND TEAROOM　　*Open daily, 9–midnight. On the corner of rue Daubenton and 39, rue Geoffroy Saint-Hilaire, opposite the Jardin des Plantes. A pretty outdoor terrace planted with jasmine, olive bushes, and fig trees where singing birds nest and play. With its dark blue mosaic of the tables and fountain and the surround of cool blue tiles, this courtyard café is pure beauty and calm.*

INSTITUT DU MONDE ARABE　　*1, rue des Fossés-Saint-Bernard, entrance through the south-side façade; daily except Mon, 10–6. A gleaming glass marvel of a building by one of France's best architects, Jean Nouvel, overlooking the Seine from the Left Bank. From the ninth-floor terrace the views of* **Île Saint-Louis** *and* **Notre-Dame** *may be the best in Paris. The Middle Eastern food served outdoors and in the cafeteria is very good. The gift shop on the main floor sells fine fabrics and pottery of exquisite Islamic designs and colors.*

JARDIN TINO ROSSI   *On Quai Saint-Bernard, along the Left Bank of the Seine. In summer, there's dancing at night. It's a peaceful little enclave, with pretty flowers, popular at lunchtime with students and faculty and visitors to the adjacent* **Musée du Sculpture en Plein Air.**

The Medicis Fountain in the Luxembourg Gardens

JARDIN DU LUXEMBOURG

ENTRANCES: place Edmond-Rostand; rue de Vaugirard;
   place Auguste-Comte
MÉTRO: Odéon
HOURS: 7:30–dusk, according to the season

June, Luxembourg Gardens:
A Sunday morning full of wind and sunlight. Over the large pool the
wind splatters the waters of the fountain; the tiny sailboats on the
windswept water and the swallows around the huge trees. Two youths
discussing: "You who believe in human dignity."

ALBERT CAMUS, *Notebooks*

Having borne witness to the life of Paris for almost four hundred years, the *Luxembourg*'s pleasures embody the beauty of that life, the harmony and ease that travelers never forget: symmetrical rows of chestnut trees; in April the pretty beds of tulips; the murmur of so many people relaxing in the sun; children jubilant before the puppet theater, then hunched over the rim of the large central octagonal basin, intent on their sailboats; above them, in the shade of the gazebo on the eastern terrace, the conviviality of music and wine and the company of friends.

The city's other life—a history of violence, catastrophe, and vicious politics—is also resonant in some of the garden's best-known features.

The **Medicis Fountain** in the northeast corner, an Italian Renaissance gem of the 1620s, was built for the Florentine Marie de Medicis, queen and then widow of *vert galant*

Henry IV. Paris despised her—in the words of André Maurois, she was "a haughty Italian—a fat blonde, handsome enough when Rubens painted her, very well pleased with herself, an authoritarian without authority." But the fountain is Marie's legacy. The stillness of the pool, shadowed by a surround of arching plane trees, contrasts with the mad narrative of the fountain sculpture: the mythological Polyphemus, the gigantic Cyclops and jealous suitor, is menacing the lovers Acis and Galatea, as if poised to devour them.

The orchard of pears and apples in the garden's southwest corner (adjacent to the rue Auguste-Comte) is a small remnant of the original settlement on the grounds of the Luxembourg: the thirteenth-century monastery garden of Carthusian monks—*Le Monastère Chartreux*—destroyed by the Terror. (Beekeeping classes are offered in the apiary.)

The *Luxembourg Palace* (another of Queen Marie's attempts to re-create her hometown in this foreign city—she had the Pitti Palace in mind), though no longer open to the public, is built on ground where the Romans once set up their military camp, now the proud house of the French senate. In the *Paris Commune* of 1871, government troops dumped the corpses of Communards in the surrounding shrubbery. During the German Occupation (1940–1944), though it served as the headquarters of the Luftwaffe and the SS, the palace was bordered—then as now—by lovely flower gardens (Nazi gardeners kept them groomed and flourishing.) In August 1944, as Allied and French troops fought to take back Paris, seven hundred Germans, ready to "fight to the last cartridge," dug trenches and hid tanks in the beds of geraniums and begonias. From the roof and cupola of the palace they kept track of the approaching regiments. The

Luxembourg Palace was the last German stronghold in Paris to surrender. When it did, on August 25, "formally and definitively, Paris was free."*

The gardens were replanted. A commemorative sculpture to the students of the Resistance stands just inside the Vaugirard gate. The statues of the royal and saintly women of France that encircle the eastern and western terraces in front of the palace were also restored. One of their number, the serenely self-possessed *Laure de Noves* (1307–1348), was neither queen nor saint. Her statue stands first in line on the western terrace, toward the southern entrance. *Laure,* who holds a book in her sleeve, was the muse of Petrarch, the woman he first saw at Mass in a church in Aquitaine—the inspiration of his sonnets, the *Canzoniere*—who had married into the de Sade family. More than four centuries later, in his prison cell at *Vincennes,* her descendent, the mad Marquis de Sade, dreamed of Laure, his ancestral idol:

> *"Her eyes had the same fire as when Petrarch sang of them. . . . I am like a child. I flung myself at her feet, calling, 'Oh, my mother!' "*†

Walking east of the eastern terrace, near the Saint-Michel entrance, you'll pass a statue of another iconic French writer, passionately unconventional, not in the slightest mad: *George Sand,* novelist, admired by Flaubert, Matthew Arnold, the Brownings, Charlotte Brontë, George Eliot, Heinrich Heine, Turgenev, and Proust. Oscar Wilde loved her for her

*Larry Collins and Dominque Lapièrre, *Is Paris Burning?*
†Francine du Plessix Gray, *At Home with the Marquis de Sade: A Life.*

compassion and generosity: "For the aristocracy of the intellect she had always the deepest veneration, but the democracy of suffering touched her more."*

West of the western terrace, the graceful *Laure de Noves* at your back, you'll pass more statues of French artists and statesmen set into the deep lawns as well as the Luxembourg regulars, for whom the word "leisure" is not an abstraction—the chess players near the *Orangerie,* the men on the *boules* courts, the children on the carousel, the readers who are everywhere. You get a sense of down-to-earth practical wisdom, of the arts of survival that have seen Parisians through centuries of wars and suffering. In the *Luxembourg,* the tough complex soul of the city comes through.

Nearby

DELACROIX MURALS, THE CHURCH OF SAINT-SULPICE *Daily, 7:30–7:30. In La Chapelle des Saints-Anges (Chapel of the Holy Angels), the first chapel on the right side of the church,* La Lutte de Jacob avec l'Ange *is one of three masterpieces.*

VILLAGE VOICE BOOKSHOP   *6, rue Princesse, two streets north of Place Saint-Sulpice, open 7 days a week. The superb English-language bookstore is presided over by owner Odile Hellier, an extraordinarily knowledgeable bookseller who also hosts regular readings by contemporary writers. www.villagevoicebookshop .com.*

INSTITUT CATHOLIQUE   *21, rue d'Assas, just off rue Vaugirard, adjacent to the Church of Saint-Joseph des Carmes. The courtyard of warm brick in a Flemish Gothic style and benches under*

* Elizabeth Harlan, *George Sand.*

plane trees is deserted in summer. It leads into the cobblestoned churchyard where 120 priests were murdered in 1792. Simone de Beauvoir studied mathematics here, and Jacques Maritain taught philosophy. Stranded in the United States during the Occupation, he taught at Princeton and wrote France My Country *(1941), a love letter to Paris: "How did it fall, this city of our hopes, this country that taught liberty to the world?"*

LA MEDITERRANÉE *2, place de l'Odéon; open every day for lunch and dinner. A first-rate seafood restaurant, facing* Le Théâtre de l'Odéon *(which has its own open-air café on the Place), a block from the rue Vaugirard entrance to the Luxembourg. Reservations required: tel 01.43.26.02.30.*

LA BASTIDE ODÉON *7, rue Corneille, a block north of the rue Vaugirard entrance to the Luxembourg. An excellent restaurant—Samuel Beckett's favorite—specializing in the food of Provence and the South of France. Reservations: reservations@bastide-Odeon.com.*

Garden of Musée Eugène Delacroix

Saint-Germain-des-Prés

MUSÉE EUGÈNE DELACROIX

ENTRANCE: 6, place de Furstemberg
MÉTRO: Saint-Germain-des-Prés
HOURS: daily, except Tues, 9:30–5

Turning left, off *rue de l'Abbaye* and into a corner of the serene **Place de Furstemberg,** you'll find the apartment and studio—now a museum—of the sublime French painter **Eugène Delacroix** (1798–1863). The museum's small shaded garden with benches is a delightful place to sit and read *The Journal of Eugène Delacroix* (on sale in the bookshop), "perhaps the greatest literary testament any painter has left."* **Delacroix** moved here from the Right Bank in 1857 so he could walk back and forth to **Saint-Sulpice,** where his murals had been commissioned for the *Chapelle des Saints-Anges* (Chapel of the Holy Angels). "I like my studio," he confided to his journal. "I work well here. The view from my small garden . . . always gives me pleasure." In this silent retreat, sitting under the trees, he planned his last masterpieces. Though his health had been poor, he told his friend George Sand that now he was

> *doing a job which has given me back the health I thought lost forever. I get up very early and hurry off to my work. I return home as late as possible and begin again the next*

*Hubert Wellington, ed., *The Journal of Eugène Delacroix.*

day. . . . Nothing gives me more pleasure than painting. . . .
I am buried in my work.

He does not mourn the loss of his social life, the nightly
dinner parties, concerts, and openings in the company of his
friends Baudelaire, Balzac, Corot, Berlioz, Mérimée, Madame
Sand, and his beloved Chopin (1810–1849).

What a good life! What a divine compensation for my
solitary state. . . . Painting, it's true, like the most exact-
ing of mistresses, harasses and torments me in a hundred
ways. . . . I have been getting up at dawn, and hurrying
off to this enchanting work as though I were rushing to
throw myself at the feet of a beloved mistress. . . . How is
it that this unending struggle revives instead of destroy-
ing me?

His memoir illuminates the passion of an artist for the
beauty of the world and the medium of his art. He writes about
mixing colors, how to achieve specific effects, his excitement
at the sight of his palette. He notes the pleasures of the *Lux-*
embourg Gardens, where he studies the shapes of leaves and
trees; he records his visits to the *Jardins des Plantes* where he
watches the animals in the Natural History museum. Reading
Delacroix, you want to see both his Paris and his paintings,
many of which, including the most famous—*Liberty Guiding*
the People, commemorating the uprising of July 28, 1830—
hang in the *Louvre* as well as in the *Musée du Petit Palais*
and the *Musée d'Orsay.*

Inside this small uncrowded museum, you find powerful
evidence of Delacroix's genius for dramatizing color in works
suffused with love for women subjects (*Jenny Le Guillou,*

Magdalen au Desert, Education de la Virgin, a drawing of George Sand), as well as for the sea, for landscape (*La Nuit ou l'Inondation*), and for wild animals (*Bacchus Fresco*). But it is outside, in the stillness of the garden, where the visitor may best contemplate the reveries of this romantic visionary. "God is within us," he writes on October 12, 1862. "He is the inner presence that causes us to admire the beautiful."

Nearby

PLACE DE FURSTEMBERG *This small square takes you by surprise. Its proportions and sophistication appear so quintessentially Parisian, so charming, especially in the dappled light of late afternoon.*

CHEZ LADURÉE *At the corner of rue Bonaparte and rue Jacob. A fine* patisserie, *specializing in* macarons, *with a gracious tearoom above the shop.*

ÉCOLE DES BEAUX-ARTS *The national school of painting and sculpture at 14, rue Bonaparte. Hours: Courtyard: Mon–Fri, 9–5; Exhibitions: Tues–Sun, 1–7. The glass-domed ceiling over the main entrance hall of terra cotta and teal blue is gorgeous. Another highlight is the* **Cour du Murier,** *the cloister of an old convent with a huge old mulberry tree—*murier*—in the center surrounded by arcades and a fountain.*

9, QUAI MALAQUAIS *Delacroix's friend George Sand lived here (1832–1836) along the Seine when she first came to Paris with her two children, in flight from a loveless marriage. Here she wrote* Lelia *and began dressing in men's clothing in order to be seated at the opera without an escort. In Sand's day, unaccompanied single women were refused admission to public places.*

THE CHURCH OF SAINT-GERMAIN-DES-PRÉS *(Saint-Germain of the Fields) Open daily 8–7. The tower dominates the* Place, *the familiar image of the Romanesque origin of what remains of a huge Benedictine monastery from the sixth century. The transition from Romanesque to early Gothic is evident in the interior, a beautiful setting for the concerts held here and posted outside. The marble statue,* Notre-Dame de Consolation, *given to the Abbey of Saint-Denis in 1340, stands in the rear of the south aisle. Fragments from the Lady Chapel (1212–1255) are scattered outside next to the church entrance in the garden of Square Laurent-Praghe, where Picasso's* Head of a Woman *also stands.*

Square Boucicaut

SQUARE BOUCICAUT

ENTRANCES: rue de Sèvres, rue de Babylone;
rue Velpeau; boulevard Raspail
MÉTRO: Sèvres-Babylone
HOURS: 8–dusk, according to the season

Whether it's the employees from *Bon Marché* relaxing on a break or the happy children on the carousel or the magnificent tall trees under a wide sky, this square has such a feeling of benevolence that you walk around soaking it up and wondering about the source. What collective memory lives in the blue air that colors this thick exotic greenery? A part of the answer is in the square's namesake: it commemorates *Aristide Boucicaut,* the founder of the elegant Bon Marché department store across the street (1852), and his wife and business partner, Marguerite Guerin Boucicaut, who inherited his fortune, one of the largest in nineteenth-century Paris, and gave most of it away to poor children, to hospitals, teachers, journalists, artists. The sculpture of *Madame Boucicaut* at the square's entrance captures the kindliness of the woman, an exceptionally generous Parisian who began life as the illegitimate daughter of a peasant.

Maybe her story has colored this space, feeds the currents of harmony—a common register in many of the squares and gardens of Paris. The children who play in them also say something about the culture of the Boucicauts' city, which the "non-stop brilliant"* twentieth-century Austrian journalist Joseph Roth describes in "The Child in Paris":

> *There are children playing in all the parks. . . . And if there is something that grown-ups are not allowed to do in one or other of the city's great parks or little green spaces, then you can bet children will be allowed to do it. In Paris children are allowed to stand on benches, squeeze between railings, clamber over fences, throw balls into flowerbeds, and pluck flowers. The French are not the ones to apply Spartan principles of education. This people, that makes and bears so few children, not only respects the child as the future of the country, the nation, the world—it quite unthinkingly loves it, the child as creature, the becoming person who is still half an animal. . . . French children behave with the ease and confidence of grown-ups. It's not so much a matter of race and blood as it is the consequence of the warm, loving, nurturing softness in the way they are brought up. The French pedagogical principle is not Spartan strictness but Roman freedom accorded to the individual disposition—it's not discipline but civilization. . . . In parks and gardens, at every fair, in open spaces on particular holidays, there are carousels for children. . . . Children are allowed to do everything: to rush ahead, . . . to feed swans, and sail little boats in ornamental ponds.*[†]

A look at the expressiveness of the ***Madame Boucicaut*** monument in the context of an Austrian's take on Parisian child-rearing—the warm, loving, nurturing softness—strikes

---

* Jeffrey Eugenides, *New York Times Book Review.*
[†] Joseph Roth, *Report from a Parisian Paradise: Essays, 1925–1939.*

a major chord of recognition. On the other hand, in the spirit of French contrariness, the nineteenth-century poet Charles Baudelaire, who felt a brotherhood with the Paris of the poor, might have felt only dislike toward this stone homage to the tradition of philanthropy: in *Les Fleurs du Mal*, "he never shows pity for the poor, nor—still worse—charitable tenderness, sentiments so widespread at the time, and that drove him into a rage."*

Nearby

BON MARCHÉ   *Partly designed by Gustave Eiffel in a brilliant glass-and-steel construction like London's Crystal Palace, it's as much a light-filled, welcoming museum as a department store, the oldest in Paris.*

HÔTEL LUTETIA   *45, boulevard Raspail at rue de Sèvres, opposite* **Square Boucicaut.** *Afternoon tea in the main salon of the Lutetia delivers the exquisite pleasure of Parisian hospitality and tasteful elegance. It's easy to see why Henry James, Matisse, and Picasso chose to stay here. During the Occupation, the Nazis installed the Gestapo; after the Liberation, Paris received its returning POWs and concentration camp survivors here. In her book* The War *(translated from the French* Le Douleur*), writer and* Résistante *Marguerite Duras (1914–1996) caught the sorrow and the muted relief of the days of repatriation. A plaque, in French, bears witness to the Lutetia's tragic role during World War II.*

JARDIN CATHERINE-LABOURÉ   *33, rue de Babylone. A tidy vegetable and flower garden on the grounds of the Sisters of Charity convent, with a lovely arbor. A haven for Parisians at lunchtime, just a few minutes' walk from Square Boucicaut.*

*Eric Hazan, *The Invention of Paris: A History in Footsteps.*

Garden behind La Clinique Saint-Jean de Dieu

JARDIN DE LA CLINIQUE
SAINT-JEAN DE DIEU

ENTRANCE: 19, rue Oudinot
MÉTRO: Saint François-Xavier
HOURS: daily, during hospital visiting hours

A pleasant receptionist in the hospital lobby will guide you to the garden: down a short hallway and through doors to the left. If you happen to visit in May and June, what awaits you outside, behind the hospital, is one of the most beautiful rose gardens in Paris. Whereas the *Bagatelle* in the *Bois du Boulogne* is a performance, the garden of **Saint-Jean de Dieu** (**Saint John of God**) feels like a state of being. If you sit far in the back, facing the fine white building that houses the clinic—it was originally the town house of Madame de la Sablière—this long view of the manicured flower beds beneath sheltering trees can make you feel as if you've come into an outdoor church sanctuary. ("The best place to find God is in a garden," said George Bernard Shaw. "You can dig for Him there.")

The healing spirituality of the hospital garden is now a theme among medical professionals and administrators who advocate making such green spaces integral parts of medical facilities. A garden, it is said, reaches a deeper level of being than the simply visual: "Here lies a reservoir of feelings, such as pleasure, displeasure, awe, fear, or fascination" with the power "to heal psychic stress."

*For in the stress of urban living, the crowding, traffic, over-
load of stimulation, lack of peace and quiet, all take their
toll. . . . Vegetation serves as a shock absorber for the human
sensory system assaulted by the sights, smells, sounds of
the city. It does not present a challenge to the senses, does
not have to be screened out, but provides an opportunity for
rest from the constant mental alertness. . . . It helps to heal
the psychological wounds congested cities inflict on their
residents.*[*]

In the garden of **Saint-Jean de Dieu** the beauty feels muted,
unaccompanied by the sounds of the more popular gardens—
the buzz of the crowds, say, on a Saturday afternoon in the
Luxembourg. Here you notice only the occasional crunch of
the pebbles on a path as a visiting friend and a patient stroll
past arm-in-arm. This would be a good place to get well,
under the balm of roses. (To your right are the high old roof-
tops of *rue Rousselet*, alongside the clinic garden, admired for
its quiet charm.)

The hospital, which specializes in surgery, was founded
by a member of the Order of Saint John of God in 1843, a fra-
ternity that opened hospitals to serve the poor and the sick
in Spain and France in 1546. Disbanded during the Terror, the
Order reestablished itself in nineteenth-century Paris. **Saint-
Jean de Dieu,** named for the founder, is no longer run by a
religious community serving the poor. It is now a private op-
eration serving the comfortable environs of *le septième*.

---

[*]Charles A. Lewis and S. Kaplan, "The Healing Power of Gardens," in *The
Meaning of Gardens: Idea, Place, and Action*, eds. Mark Francis and Ran-
dolph T. Hester.

Nearby

THE GARDEN OF THE CINÉMA LA PAGODE   *57 bis, rue de Babylone. This Japanese garden, with its stone dragons, lions, Buddhas, birds, and a ginkgo biloba, is the entrance to one of the best independent art cinémas in Paris.*

GARDENS OF UNESCO   *7, place de Fontenoy. Featuring the work of renowned Japanese American sculptor and landscape architect* **Isamu Noguchi.** *Reserve a visit through an answering service: 33.(0).145.681.060.*

AVENUE DE BRETEUIL   *A long mall of lawns lined with trees and benches, the golden dome of Les Invalides always in view.*

The Sculpture Garden of Musée Rodin

MUSÉE RODIN

ENTRANCE: 77, rue de Varenne

MÉTRO: Varenne

HOURS: Tues–Sun, Apr–Sept, 9:30–6:45; Oct–Mar,
9:30–5

The spacious gardens can be visited independently of the museum, the most popular in Paris dedicated to a single artist. In Rodin's day, this was a wild park. A makeover in 1993 established a highly designed layout well suited to the architecture of the museum, an elegant eighteenth-century mansion. A variety of trees—lindens, chestnuts, trimmed box trees, clipped yews—complement the generous flower beds and a large pool. The entire composition frames the mansion's south façade, where Rodin (1840–1917) had his studio. The trees you can see from his studio windows would have delighted him. As he wrote in his poetic *Cathedrals of France*:

> *Trees bring order and animation to everything . . . like archangels, [they] bow their heads to one another, their wings unfurled, vertical against the sky.*"*

The most powerful presences in the garden are the sculptures, scattered about in the open, others discreetly set among holly bushes and other greenery. Along one path, thick with plantings, you suddenly come upon *The Thinker* (and all the

* Auguste Rodin, *Cathedrals of France*.

thinking tourists posing for cameras in front of him). Elsewhere are *The Burghers of Calais; The Gates of Hell,* influenced by the imagery of Dante's *Divine Comedy* and Michelangelo's *Last Judgment* in the Sistine Chapel; and in the pool, **Ugolino and His Children.** Inside the museum are sketches and models Rodin made for his masterpiece, *Honoré de Balzac.* There's a copy in the garden; the original, which Parisians despised at first, stands on a pedestal under trees on a median north of the intersection of boulevard du Montparnasse and boulevard Raspail in **Montparnasse.**

In late afternoon, as the sun fades slowly in the west behind the nearby gold dome of *Les Invalides* and the Eiffel Tower seems to touch the pink sky, the gardens feel animated by the spirit of the artists who had their studios in the mansion with Rodin as well as by the city that at once inspired and enraged them. One of the artists who shared his space was the sculptor Camille Claudel (1864–1943), Rodin's collaborator and lover for eleven years. Their breakup, like their affair, was tempestuous, having lifelong tragic consequences for Claudel. (The movie *Camille Claudel*, with Isabelle Adjani as Claudel and Gérard Depardieu as Rodin, tells the bitter story.)

It was Rodin's friend, the poet Rainer Maria Rilke (1875–1926), who first told him about the available studio space in what was then called Hôtel Biron, and who later worked as his office assistant.* (Rilke's novel, *The Notebooks of Malte Laurids Brigge*, completed after his first stay in Paris in 1908, tells the story of his survival in those early years in the alienating yet supremely alive city.) After Rodin's death, Rilke wrote a brilliant monograph about his friend. His insights

---

*Ruth Butler, *The Shape of Genius.*

achieve a rich texture when contemplated in the silence of this garden in late afternoon:

> *Indeed, it is an underlying patience in Rodin which renders him so great, a silent, superior forbearance resembling the wonderful patience and kindness of Nature. . . . "One must not hurry," said Rodin . . . He possessed the quiet perseverance of men who are necessary.**

Nearby

THE GARDEN CAFÉ   *A treasure, tucked away under the hedges, along a shady path.*

BASILICA OF SAINT-CLOTILDE   *23, rue las Casas. Métro, Solferino. A lovely nineteenth-century mock Gothic cathedral, where César Franck was the organist for fifty years, and now the setting for glorious choral concerts (Brahms, Mendelssohn, Bach, Fauré). Schedules available at www.sainte-clotilde.com. Edith Wharton, who lived nearby at 53, rue de Varenne, loved the sound of Saint-Clotilde's church bells.*

SQUARE SAMUEL ROUSSEAU   *Directly across from the church, a lively green space in the afternoons, full of children and Parisians taking their time. There is a statue of César Franck and a sculpture of a woman reading to a child.*

THE SQUARE   *21, rue Saint-Dominique. A good restaurant with a nice bar, convenient for dinner before the concerts, which start at 8:45. Outdoor seating has a view of the square and Saint-Clotilde.*

---

*Rainer Maria Rilke, *Letters on Life*, ed. Ulrich Baer.

Square Récamier

SQUARE RÉCAMIER

ENTRANCE: rue de Sèvres and rue Récamier
MÉTRO: Sèvres-Babylone
HOURS: early morning–dusk

Perhaps the best-kept secret of the city's small squares, *Square Récamier* is hard to find. Off to the right as you walk west on the north side of *rue de Sèvres,* just past its intersection with *rue des Saints-Pères,* you'll come upon the narrow pedestrian *rue Récamier* (and its fine restaurant, Le Récamier, where President and Mrs. Obama dined), which leads directly to the square. A staircase under the drapery of a pergola takes you down past a small waterfall and pool, into a valley-like romantic space hung with the spreading branches of trees, overgrown rhododendron, and rock gardens thick with ivy, myrtle, and, in season, white tulips and buttercups. The surrounding architecture is as tasteful as the garden. With its hidden-away corners and nooks where it's possible to sit unobserved from other parts of the square, it's also a discreet place.

The square's namesake, *Juliette Récamier* (1777–1849), is remembered for her exquisite beauty and grace—her portrait by David hangs in the Louvre; Gérard's in the Carnavalet—but most of all she is defined by her romantic "friendships" which brought a certain frisson to the hermetic world of the literary salon. Madame Récamier's salon was the first one to reopen its doors after the Revolution. Of all her admirers, it was Chateaubriand who offered the most passionate adoration. Every morning he wrote her a love letter: "In looking at your divine beauty one feels transported, and it robs death of its shadows of gloom." Every afternoon he went to visit her.*

Though she was Germaine de Staël's closest woman friend, and the model for the main character of her novel *Corinne, ou l'Italie* (1807), she was also the confidante of Benjamin Constant, de Staël's longtime lover. Their nasty breakup did not destroy the bond between Constant and Julie.

She lived at Abbaye au Bois, a large old building in rue de Sèvres overlooking a pretty garden, preserved today as **Square Récamier.** She is described as "a small, delicate woman with a timid, whispering voice; she adopted a manner at once frigidly chaste and playfully coquettish."[†] She remained a virgin until her forties. When the afternoons spent flirting with Chateaubriand eventually turned into passionate nights, the liaison between them would last for the rest of her life.

Napoleon exiled her from Paris for a time along with her friend Germaine de Staël, who had disapproved loudly and in print of his politics. "Women should stick to knitting," Napoleon responded. "Paris is . . . where I live. I don't want anyone there who doesn't like me."[‡]

Nearby

POILÂNE   *8, rue Cherche-Midi. One of the oldest and best Parisian bakeries, offering the legendary large round loaves of brown bread, butter cookies, and nut rolls.*

---

* Delia Austrian, *Juliette Récamier.*
† Francine du Plessix Gray, *Madame de Staël: The First Modern Woman.*
‡ Ibid.

THÉÂTRE VIEUX-COLOMBIER *21, rue Vieux-Colombier. Part of the Comédie Française, a popular theater—where Sartre's* No Exit *was first performed in 1944—dedicated to contemporary repertoire, with an inviting bar and old stage sets located in the lobby.*

The Eiffel Tower at the western edge of the Champ de Mars

CHAMP DE MARS

ENTRANCE: place Joffre and avenue de la Motte Picquet,
  across from l'École Militaire
MÉTRO: École Militaire
HOURS: Open 24 hours

The Eiffel Tower, rising over the Seine at the western edge of this long slice of green, commemorates the shock heard round the world in 1789, the storming of the Bastille on July 14. Gustave Eiffel opened his Tower in 1889 in honor of the centenary of the French Revolution, the most radical and transformative political event in modern Western history.

The Revolution's first anniversary was celebrated here on the vast expanse of *Champ de Mars*—the "Martial Fields"—also the setting, in 1794, for Robespierre's first and only festival of the Supreme Being—*Fête de l'Être Suprême*. Having outlawed Catholicism, the Revolutionary Convention proclaimed "a deistic substitute for the Christian God" and assembled a procession of thousands to worship the "Author of Nature."* Citizens, soldiers, cavalry, politicians, starting at the Tuileries, marched across the Seine and down the Left Bank behind floats and bands and choruses to climb an artificial mountain and declaim their patriotism at the altar to the Supreme Being. Four generations later, in the same place, Gustave Eiffel, an engineer of genius, "wrought a monument

---

*Frederick Brown, *For the Soul of France: Culture Wars in the Age of Dreyfus*.

to the god of scientific progress. Where the mountain had stood, a tower rose."* The Revolution's bicentenary was commemorated by the sculpture *Monument des Droits de l'Homme et du Citoyen* (*Monument to the Rights of Man and Citizens*) in the vicinity of La Bonbonnière de Laura et Marie and the small café behind the children's carousel toward the east end of the field.

Originally a local market garden, and later used for military exercises from the time of Louis XV to Napoleon, **Champ de Mars** now serves as a place to relax. Couples lie in the grass, people read and sleep, children run, polite French poodles jump, gardeners prune rosebushes—still blooming in November—and in the bright pink light of an evening in June, joggers jog along the bordering tree-lined paths. There's music on hot summer nights when the grass is crowded with picnickers and the park stays open round the clock. Across from l'École Militaire on the eastern end—directly opposite the Eiffel Tower—the magnificent glass Peace Wall,† incised with messages of peace from all over the world, in many languages, expresses hope for the world's future. In the far distance, more than a kilometer away, its lattice sides twinkling with champagne lights after dusk, the Tower bears witness to one man's imagination and his century's dream of progress.

Nowadays Robespierre's bloody reign feels remote to the point of oblivion, as does the scorn that Gustave Eiffel got for his troubles in 1889. The day his Tower opened, he climbed the 2,731 steps to the top and unfurled the French flag. But the protest against him and his iron marvel was bitter: *la Tour Eiffel* was denounced as an "odious column of bolted

* Brown, *For the Soul of France.*

† Clara Halter and Jean-Michel Wilmotte, *Peace Wall.* www.murpourlapaix.org.

metal."* The protesting Parisians, artists in the main, preferred their monuments carved in stone.

Nearby

GARDENS OF THE MUSÉE DU QUAI BRANLY   *56, quai Branly; Tues–Sun, 10–6:30; Thurs, until 9:30. The work of architect Jean Nouvel, opened in 2000, the museum of ethnography and ethnology presents the art of Oceania, Asia, Africa, and the Americas. The outdoor restaurant, Les Ombres, faces the delightfully unmanicured gardens of tall grasses, bamboo, and banana and palm trees. It also has views of the Eiffel Tower. A footbridge, Passerelle Debilly, connects quai Branly to the Right Bank.*

AMERICAN CHURCH IN PARIS   *65, quai d'Orsay. The notice board of this Protestant church and community center has all sorts of useful information about events, concerts, and services for English-speaking visitors. www.acparis.org.*

---

* Brown, *For the Soul of France.*

Sculpture of Saint-Exupéry, Square Santiago du Chili

SQUARE SANTIAGO DU CHILI

ENTRANCE: boulevard de la Tour-Maubourg and rue
  Grenelle
MÉTRO: La Tour-Maubourg
HOURS: dawn to dusk

Perhaps the greenest and sweetest-smelling grass in Paris early on a June morning after a night of steady rain covers this small triangle of a square; on such a morning it feels almost preternaturally alive. It's surrounded by the wide lawns of the Esplanade of *Les Invalides*, and from its benches you face the gleaming and elegant *Église du Dôme*. Though it's bordered by boulevard de la Tour-Maubourg and rue Grenelle and a few bistros, somehow the square is an oasis of peace. The particular brightness of the summer morning light—the feeling of sky and openness—tells you the Seine is near, even if you don't know it from a map.

The most compelling attraction is the sculpted bust of ***Antoine de Saint-Exupéry*** (1900–1944). One of the first professional airplane pilots at the age of twenty-six, ***Saint-Exupéry***'s renowned, most indelible gift to France was his writing. His books are now classics of French and world literature. Some draw on his flying experiences: *Southern Mail*, *Wind, Sand and Stars*, *Night Flight*, *Flight to Arras*.*He wrote his best-known work, *The Little Prince*, in New York while in

*Antoine de Saint-Exupéry, *Wartime Writings 1939–1944*. Introduction by Anne Morrow Lindbergh.

exile during the German Occupation. According to biographer Stacy Schiff, he was about as unconventional as only a great man can be: an adventurer who loved the natural world and discovering new places despite the danger. He was also a visionary for whom the interior life, private, mysterious, inexhaustible, was the most significant of all human experiences.*

The bust is placed here because when he wasn't in the air or in the African desert, Saint-Exupéry lived nearby, in rue de Chanaleilles, and later in an art deco apartment at 15, place Vauban (marked with a plaque), at the rear of Les Invalides, near the entrance to the museum—a short walk south along boulevard de la Tour-Maubourg and left into avenue de Tourville. Though he belonged to the literary community of *Saint-Germain*, drinking and talking and writing at *Chez Lipp* and *Deux Magots*, he felt himself an outsider in Paris and disliked what he considered the "small world" of the capital's cultural elites. To sit in this pretty square (named for the Chilean embassy, which is nearby) and read Schiff's superb book about this brave and complicated man—"he lived so much tangled up in paradox"—is to come close to an enigmatic pilgrim soul and thereby to the interior heart of the city he both loved and hated.

It's fine, too, to just sit and smell the grass and flowers under the wide blue sky.

Nearby

CHURCH GARDEN OF SAINT-JEAN   *Evangelical Lutheran church 147, rue de Grenelle. The small lovely flower gardens—*

---

* Stacy Schiff, *Saint-Exupéry: A Biography.*

and benches and trees—extend around the church, providing another oasis in which it's hard to believe there's a city just beyond the front courtyard. The only sound comes through the windows of the school buildings behind the church. Sometimes the children sing.

Jardin Atlantique - Gare Montparnasse

JARDIN ATLANTIQUE

ENTRANCES: from Gare Montparnasse; or from place des
Cinq Martyrs du Lycée Buffon
MÉTRO: Montparnasse
HOURS: daily, 8:30–9:30

A garden has been planted on the roof of one of the largest train stations in Paris. It's laid out on a long concrete slab that has been transformed into an ingenious green oasis with a maritime theme, since the trains from *Gare Montparnasse* run to the Atlantic coast and Brittany. Walking south down the central lawn, you have the choice of spending time in a forest of five hundred trees—weeping willows, pines, oaks, and evergreens—and plants—holly, yew, ferns, and hostas—or sitting inside the sand dunes area, among the reeds and tall wild grasses moving in the wind, just as you'd find on the French Atlantic coast. Most incredible—since the tracks of a huge train station are just below—is the Room of Silence or the Garden for Meditation. Or if you prefer the sounds of nature, there are small waterfalls and fountains in the Room of Moisture. Teenagers hang out on the sun deck, near a few tennis courts and Ping-Pong tables. Each of the thematic gardens has an originality sparked by the imagination and boldness of architects François Brun and Michel Pena, who opened the 8.5 acres of *Jardin Atlantique* in 1994.

At the north end, back toward the stairway leading down to the station, is an informative and moving memorial to French courage. First, the *Musée Jean-Moulin* covers the

French Resistance to the German Occupation (1940–1944), using documentary evidence connected with its greatest hero, Jean Moulin (1899–1943), an agent from Charles de Gaulle's London-based Free French, who unified the many secret networks into the ragged army of the French Resistance. In 1943, he was captured and tortured by the notorious Klaus Barbie, who beat him to death. "He who knew everything betrayed nothing," as his sister put it.[*] André Malraux's speech upon the transfer of Moulin's ashes to the Panthéon in 1964 is one of the most famous and powerful in French history.[†] The museum is located in Montparnasse because it was Moulin's favorite *quartier*: an artist himself who had an apartment and many artist-friends in the neighborhood, he spent a lot of time in its cafés and his friends' homes.

The highly informative *Memorial of the Liberation of Paris* focuses on *Maréchal Philippe Leclerc,* the leader of the French Second Armored Division, who, with his American allies, won the fight for the Liberation of Paris in 1944 and made *Gare Montparnasse* his headquarters during the days before the final victory on August 25. It was here, too, that General von Choltitz, commander of the German army of Occupation, signed the cease-fire agreement.

Nearby

TOUR MONTPARNASSE   *Open every day, 9:30–11. Entrance on rue de l'Arrivée, in front of the* **Gare Montparnasse.** *The lift to the top—the fifty-sixth floor—of the city's tallest building takes thirty-eight seconds, ending in an unforgettable panoramic overview*

---

[*] Patrick Marnham, *Resistance and Betrayal: The Death and Life of the Greatest Hero of the French Resistance*.

[†] www.oocities.org/resistancehistory/malraux.

of the city's parks and squares, the sparkling Seine, the white lines of boulevards, the spires and domes and palaces. Through headphones, the chansons of Josephine Baker, Charles Trenet, Georges Brassens, Jacques Brel, Mistinguett, and others accompany the view. Beyond the walls of photographs of the bridges and hotels of Paris, there's an open-air terrace.

RUE DE LA GAÎTÉ   *Since the eighteenth century, this has been the street of popular commercial theaters, cabarets, and dance halls: for instance, the Bobino music hall; la Gaîté, where Colette performed; and Théâtre Montparnasse.*

RUE DELAMBRE   *Where Gauguin lived in a hotel, leads into* **place Pablo Picasso** *and* **boulevard Montparnasse,** *the crossroads where from the terrace of* **Le Dôme** *(one of Sartre and de Beauvoir's favorite cafés) you can see Rodin's* Balzac *on a pedestal across boulevard Montparnasse under trees.*

Sculpture Garden, Musée Zadkine

MUSÉE ZADKINE

ENTRANCE: 100 bis, rue d'Assas
MÉTRO: Vavin
HOURS: Tues–Sun, 10–6

The painter and sculptor *Ossip Zadkine* (1890–1967), born in Belarus, the son of a Jewish father and Scottish mother, came to Paris from Russia in 1909 by way of a London art school. At first he lived at *La Ruche,* an artists' community, but finding it too confining, he moved on, though remaining a regular among the artists and poets of the Russian diaspora in the café worlds of *Port-Royal* and *la Rotonde* in *Montparnasse.* He counted among his colleagues the painters Soutine, Chagall, Kandinsky, and Survage. Auguste Rodin was a strong influence on his early sculpture. Zadkine was one of the shining lights of the School of Paris, composed of many foreign artists who settled in Paris. Achieving recognition in the 1920s, in 1928 Zadkine bought the small home and studio that is now a museum filled with his sculptures in stone and wood and bronze and numerous paintings. "Come and see my Assas folly," he wrote to a friend, "and you'll understand just how much a man's life can be changed by a pigeon loft, by a tree." You enter his "folly"—a gift to the city after his death—through a small sculpture garden shaded by tall birch trees; in late afternoon they filter the falling sunlight as it moves beyond the garden walls. Since Zadkine's retreat is well off the beaten track, most days you'll find the peace to contemplate the beauty of his sculptures, *Melancholy* and *The Birth of Venus,* among many others. Inside the museum you can see the range of his styles: from early primitivism and cubism through expressionism and abstraction.

Zadkine's retreat is a small piece of the Russian diaspora that followed the Bolshevik Revolution of 1917 when about four hundred thousand of the Russian "intelligentsia"—artists and writers—who left their homeland emigrated mostly to Berlin and Paris,[*] bringing their genius with them. Nina Berberova, Zadkine's contemporary, arrived in Paris in 1925 and stayed until 1950, when she moved to the United States. The Assas dovecote is a nice setting for discovering her fiction of post-revolutionary Russians—for instance, her masterpiece, *The Accompanist.* Zadkine had many writers among his friends, Russian and others; he himself was a serious and respected poet. Indeed, the subtlety and silence of his sculptures suggest the inspiration and power of poetry itself.

Nearby

MUSÉE BOURDELLE   *16, rue Antoine-Bourdelle, a short distance from Gare Montparnasse through the underground passage to Place Bienvenue. Open Tues–Sun, 10–6. This museum consists of the house, studio, and garden (where you'll find Zadkine's huge bronzes) of sculptor Antoine Bourdelle (1861–1929), a student of Rodin who went on to work alongside him and who has been called "the man who invented modernism."*[†]

CLOSERIE DES LILAS   *171, boulevard Montparnasse. A favored café of writers and poets such as Baudelaire, Verlaine,*

[*] Valerian Obolensky, *Russians in Exile: The History of the Diaspora.* On the Web: Valobel.blogspot.com./russians-in-exile-history.

[†] Gregor Dallas, *"Montparnasse,"* in *Métro Stop Paris.*

Gautier, and Zola, and painters Manet, Gauguin, and other impressionists. Such poets as Max Jacob and Apollinaire used to read their work here on Tuesday evenings called "Vers et Prose."

MONTPARNASSE CEMETERY   *Enter from boulevard Edgar Quinet (daily, 8–6) and pick up a map from the guardhouse at the entrance to guide you to the graves of the famous. A quiet place, with few visitors wandering in the shade of the linden trees. Here lie Sartre and Simone de Beauvoir, side by side; also Samuel Beckett, Baudelaire, Captain Dreyfus, and Ossip Zadkine.*

The Campanile, Parc Georges-Brassens, Montparnasse

PARC GEORGES-BRASSENS

ENTRANCE: 36 bis, rue des Morillons
MÉTRO: Convention
HOURS: dawn–dusk

On the map it may look far from the city center, but after you exit the métro, the delightful *Parc Georges-Brassens* is only a ten-minute walk away on rue Dantzig and left into rue Morillons at the Préfecture de Police building on the corner. Farther on, the main entrance opens wide beneath a presiding pair of bronze bulls. Ahead of you is a modest and diverse loveliness, but the bulls remain an iconic reminder of the nineteen-acre parkland's former life as the grounds of the old Vaugirard slaughterhouses, where 110,000 cows and steers, 70,000 calves, 500,000 sheep, and 80,000 pigs were slaughtered and butchered annually. Before 1977, when this land was transformed into a park, it reeked.

In deference to that past, stroll first toward the left as you cross the main plaza, past the round pool, the fountains and ducks, the benches and trees, until you come to the *fragrance garden,* planted with over eighty species of aromatic and medicinal plants; when they're in bloom, the scent perfumes the air, a pleasant revision of history. Behind the *campanile*— atop the building where the beasts were once auctioned off, no doubt shrieking and groaning—as you climb the winding path up a small hill, you pass an apiary and cross a stream bordered with pine and birch trees; spread over the hilltop are beehives and a small terraced vineyard. The path continues past lush beds of heather, rhododendron, azalea, wildflowers, and magnolia trees. Then you enter a shady wooded area, a haven of silence moving with breezes out of tall maple trees. The children's rock-climbing area and the playgrounds are tucked away elsewhere. To the south is a theater, with bleachers, in the shape of a pyramid.

The pleasures continue as you circle back toward the east, in the vicinity of *rue Brancion*. What was once the old horse market is now the venue for the Saturday and Sunday book fairs: book dealers assemble their tables of rare, used, and new books, and the book-loving connoisseurs who show up faithfully make it worth their while. It's a thriving scene animated with good spirits and the quiet attention of book lovers. The words of rock musician Patti Smith, lover of Paris and winner of the 2010 National Book Award for *Just Kids*, resonate beautifully in this setting:

> *Please, no matter how we advance technologically, please don't abandon the book—there is nothing in our material world more beautiful than the book.*

It doesn't seem in much danger among the weekend book buyers or the people relaxing in *Georges-Brassens* on one bright golden afternoon in mid-October: on the benches, on the grass, to a man, to a woman, everyone had their nose in a book (or newspaper).

How pleased *Georges Brassens* (1921–1981) would be. The singer, songwriter, and poet—the sculpted bust of his handsome head stands to the east near the site of the book fairs—studied and loved the poems of Apollinaire, François Villon, and Louis Aragon, which he set to music. Singers

Charles Trenet, Tino Rossi, and Ray Ventura were his idols. A high school dropout from the provinces—he called himself a "thug"—he arrived penniless in Paris and spent his time in the library. During World War II, the Germans deported him to a forced-labor camp. Going AWOL, he hid in a friend's flat nearby, without running water, gas, or electricity, and studied Baudelaire, Verlaine, and Victor Hugo. He wrote songs, such as "L'Auvergnat," praising the protectors of the poor and mocking the pettiness of the bourgeoisie. Ordinary Parisians adored his singing and the countercultural lyrics of his 250 songs advocating social justice, friendship, and love. A mural portrait of him hangs in the *Porte des Lilas* métro station, along with the lyrics of his song, *"La Porte des Lilas,"* which plays in the film of the same name by René Clair.

Nearby

AU BEHIER D'ARGENT *Restaurant and café at 5, place Jacques Marette across from the main entrance of the park. A quiet and pretty prospect, with excellent coffee.*

VILLA SANTOS-DUMONT *Bressens moved to 42, rue Santos-Dumont in 1968, a garden home along this leafy green cul-de-sac.*

LA RUCHE *(The Beehive) Off rue Dantzig, to 2, Passage rue Dantzig, to the right of Café Dantzig. The name comes from the design, by Gustave Eiffel, of the artists' studios laid out around a staircase in the shape of cells in a beehive. Opened in 1902 as a home for refugee artists from central Europe, it offered space to painters and sculptors—Chagall, Leger, Archipenko, Soutine, Modigliani, Zadkine—and poets—Apollinaire and Max Jacob—in the years when the fifteenth* arrondissement *in Montparnasse was the setting of a new art scene, sometimes called the School of Paris. Chagall and André Malraux saved the studios from demolition in the 1960s. You can look through the locked gate into an old mossy courtyard, and sometimes are allowed entrance.*

Parc Montsouris

PARC MONTSOURIS

ENTRANCES: avenue Reille; rue Gazan; rue de la Cité; boulevard Jourdan

MÉTRO: Porte d'Orléans; RER line B to Cité Universitaire

HOURS: 8–7, according to the season

B on Weekend! You hear that all over Paris on Friday afternoons. Saturdays, you realize these are words Parisians translate into action. In late morning they start pouring into the streets, lining up at cafés, and sprawling on the grass and under the trees of, for example, the beautiful and large *Parc Montsouris* on the southern border of *Montparnasse.* The winding paths of Montsouris take you up, down, and around the mounds of lawn. They circle the waterfall above the artificial lake, lead past dense and deep groves of flowering shrubbery—forsythia, jasmine, hydrangea—and eventually move into shade under century-old trees. The bronze sculptures of lovers, of tigers battling snakes, of wild animals that decorate the sloping lawns are wonderful. The city's meteorological observatory is housed on the western side, with the day's weather predictions posted on the door. Near the southern entrance—the green campus of *Cité Universitaire* is across the boulevard—up on a stagelike platform, you can observe a class practicing Tahtib, Egyptian martial arts, on Saturday mornings. It's a kind of stick fighting or stick fencing accompanied by bass drums that originated along the Nile four thousand years ago.

When Jean-Charles Adolphe Alphand, Napoleon III's

director of public works in charge of landscape architecture, opened *Montsouris* in 1878, carrying out Georges-Eugène Haussmann's plan to create green spaces around the city, he had to close quarries and clear dozens of windmills before the area's fifty acres could be transformed into an English-style park, all winding contours and random flower beds, so different from the perfect symmetry of the Tuileries. The Englishness of *Montsouris* extends beyond its borders. In the charming narrow side streets and culs-de-sac off its western border, as you stroll through square de Montsouris, rue du Parc Montsouris, and rue Braque (the painter Georges Braque lived at number 6), passing the handsome old houses of timber and stone wrapped in wisteria and ivy and fronted with gardens of roses and lilac in season, you're reminded of a small country village, Bucklebury, say, in West Berkshire.

Nearby

JARDIN ZAC ALÉSIA MONTSOURIS *A few blocks to the northwest, across avenue Reille, this small park holds the remains of two aqueducts, one Gallo-Roman, the other from the time of Catherine de Medicis, discovered during the construction of the garden, which opened in 2005. A large space* ondule— *undulating—between the pretty community garden on the hill-side and the children's play area near the street makes this an unusual and appealing park design.*

LA BUTTE AUX CAILLES* *Follow avenue Reille from Mont-souris into rue Tolbiac, bearing left up into the hilly area—the* butte—*of the village-like neighborhood of* **Butte aux Cailles.**

*Helene Hatte and Valerie Addach, *Promenades dans le Quartier des Gobelins et la Butte-aux-Cailles*.

From **Place de la Commune,** *where heavy fighting took place in the civil war of 1871, continue to explore the narrow cobblestone streets, especially rue Daviel in Little Alsace, past the workers' villas—numbers 7 and 10—with their small, intimate courtyards and bright flower gardens. Also look for* **rue des Cinq Diamant:** *Les Amis de la Commune (no 46) preserves the memory of the communards with posters and books for sale (*The Letters of Louise Michel*).* **Chez Gladines,** *at 30, rue des Cinq Diamant, serves good French Basque meals in an informal but crowded setting. Then bear left at Square Jonas to the hillside* **Jardin Georges-Brassai,** *with its profusion of flowering trees in spring. Back toward the Place d'Italie métro is the pretty* **Square Henri-Rousselle** *with the excellent* **La Butte Aveyronnaise** *restaurant just off it at 12,* rue de la Butte aux Cailles.

CITÉ FLORALE *Off rue Brillat-Savarin (36–38), south of rue Tolbiac along rue Bobilot. The little streets are named for the flowers in the front gardens of the charming small houses:* rue des Orchides, rue des Glycines, rue des Liserons, rue des Iris, *and* Square des Mimosas. *So fragrant after a morning of light rain, this neighborhood is a hidden treasure, utterly removed from the beaten track.*

SQUARE RENÉ LE GALL *Descend the staircase of rue Eugène Atget from Jardin Georges-Brassai, cross boulevard Auguste Blanqui, and continue down rue Corvisart to the entrance. The friendly and busy square, tree-lined and lush with greenery along its long rectangular esplanade, is named for a city councilman killed by the Nazis in 1942. Métro Les Gobelins is nearby.*

Parc de Bagatelle, Bois de Boulogne

Western Paris

BOIS DE BOULOGNE:
PARC DE BAGATELLE

ENTRANCES: allée de Longchamp; route de Sèvres-â-
Neuilly
MÉTRO: Porte Maillot, then bus 244; Pont de Neuilly,
then bus 43
HOURS: 10–6; winter, 10–5

In late May over a thousand varieties of roses bloom in the
Rose Garden of the *Parc de Bagatelle,* creating a vast canvas of pastels and bold reds between the Seine and a small
hill topped by a pagoda. As you walk the perfumed paths of
the *rosaires* and read the poetic names affixed to each bush—
"Daydream," a hot pink—you may enjoy the cultural associations of the garden. Among the famous women of Paris
who reveled in roses were the legendary mistresses of Louis
XV, Madame de Pompadour (flowers—specifically, roses—
were one of the passions of her life), and her successor, Madame du Barry—"the only woman in France who can make
me forget that I am in my sixties," said the king. Empress Josephine, the wife of Napoleon, and later the chaste Empress
Eugénie, wife of Napoleon's nephew, Napoleon III, who, like
his uncle, reigned as self-declared emperor, also preferred
roses to all other flowers: both cherished them as emblems of
romantic love. (Paris, the city of romance, is rich in rose gardens. They include *Square Georges-Cain, Parc de Belleville,*
and *Clinique Saint-Jean de Dieu.* Madame de Pompadour's
rose mania shows up as a riot of floral *jouissance* in the room

by Boucher, her protégé, in The Frick Collection in New York City.

The *Bois*—or woodlands—that surround the *Bagatelle* originally served as a royal hunting ground and a "discreetly leafy" romantic hideout, to quote Alistair Horne.* The 2,200 acres of beech, linden, cedar, chestnuts, elm, and fifteen thousand mulberry trees include remnants of the ancient *Forêt de Rouvray*, to which Haussmann and Alphand gave a more designed landscape in the nineteenth century. But always this bucolic getaway on the western edge of Paris—where fashionable people, women in their carriages and men on horseback, went to see and to be seen—offered opportunities for hedonistic orgies and secret sexual encounters. Gustave Flaubert and his lover, the poet Louise Colet, one of the models for Emma Bovary, took long hansom cab rides in the *Bois*. In 1846, according to Colet's biographer, during the fireworks of the sixteenth anniversary of the 1830 Citizens Revolution, their cab

> *proceeds toward the Bois de Boulogne, whose alleys are draped with luminous garlands. The coach moves slowly amid a raging lightning storm, amid burst of flashing rockets, and patriotic shouting; the thunder is deafening throughout Paris, flashes of lightning seem to celebrate their lust. As Gustave would write Louise a few days later: "They blazed for us . . . like a flaming beginning of love."*

Jean-Paul Sartre "is certain that Louise's and Gustave's first lovemaking took place then and there, inside that black hansom cab."[†]

* Alistair Horne, *Seven Ages of Paris*.
[†] Francine du Plessix Gray, *Rage and Fire: A Life of Louise Colet*.

Marcel Proust, who played in the ***Bois*** as a child, resurrected it in *Swann's Way*. The fashionable courtesans of Colette's *Chéri* staged their promenades and *liaisons érotiques* in the shelter of the ancient trees, their spirited rendezvous the backdrop of the opening scene of the film *Gigi*. Director Robert Bresson takes a more satiric view of the women of western Paris in his 1945 film *Les Dames du Bois de Boulogne*. The 2001 novel *The Sexual Life of Catherine M*, by Catherine Millet, describes the nightlife of prostitutes and groupies in the area of the Porte Dauphine entrance, northeast of the gardens, descriptions not taken as fictional.

In the daylight hours, this vast parkland of lakes, lawns, flowers, groves, waterfalls, bridges, duck ponds, race courses, playgrounds, cafés, and restaurants—and a Shakespeare garden—is a comfort zone for Parisians and tourists who want a break from the noise and air of the city. Here you can rent boats and bicycles, play the horses, picnic, stroll, or lie in the sun.

And from every winding path of the ***Parc de Bagatelle,*** night and day, you can smell the roses.

L'ORANGERIE   *In the eighteenth century, every great house had its* orangerie. *In this lovely classical building within the* **Parc de Bagatelle,** *which is perpendicular to the original house, the Bagatelle (built by the brother of Louis XVI, the future Charles X), there are exhibits of paintings and sculpture May to October; in the summer months there are nightly concerts of Chopin.*

PARC DES SERRES D'AUTEUIL   *3, avenue de la Porte d'Auteuil. Métro, Porte d'Auteuil (10–7, according to the season).*

Renovated in 1999, this is one of the most magnificent garden structures in Europe, made of metal and glass and greenery. There is a rare silence here, though the innovative green space is popular with Parisians.

NEUILLY-SUR-SEINE *The sidewalks along the quiet shady streets of this well-bred suburb, only minutes from the **Bois** and the center of Paris, are planted with trees. Pretty flower boxes decorate the windows of the comfortable modern apartments. The Seine runs along the southern border. Kandinsky lived here, as did Nicolas Sarkozy before he moved to the Élysée.*

Balzac's cottage and garden, Passy

MAISON DE BALZAC

ENTRANCE: 47, rue Raynouard
MÉTRO: Passy, via no. 6 métro
HOURS: Tues–Sun, 10–6 (closed Mon, holidays)

The number 6 métro—the aerial métro—is the best scenic ride in Paris. The track is elevated after Bercy. Take it to Passy, to Balzac's off-the-beaten-track garden, which served its famous resident as an actual hideaway. Here on the hillside of once rural Passy, the writer *Honoré de Balzac* (1799–1850), whose finances were as complicated as the plots of his novels, evaded his creditors and escaped out the back door down into rue Berton when they caught up with him. The walk up the hill from the *Passy* métro station, "hidden behind chestnut trees and roses, and the tracks leading towards the *Pont de Bir-Hakeim . . .* famous from *Last Tango in Paris,*"* leads to *rue Raynouard* and, after a five-minute walk, to the entrance to Balzac's cottage; once you descend into the garden you feel as if you've left far behind the city and the monotonous suburb, the sixteenth *arrondissement*—"snob Passy" to the protagonist of Alan Furst's novel of Occupied Paris, *Red Gold*.

When in bloom, the luxuriantly fat hydrangeas and rhodo-dendrons and rosebushes—with chairs and a fine sculpture of Balzac tucked discreetly along the winding paths—make the place a delightful sanctuary for both pilgrims and readers deep into, say, *Cousin Bette* (1846), one of the masterpieces

---

*Eric Hazan, *The Invention of Paris: A History in Footsteps.*

Balzac wrote here. As the self-defined "secretary of French society," he wrote almost one hundred novels, a chronicle entitled *La Comédie Humaine* (*The Human Comedy*). He began writing at midnight, continued until midday, fueled by black coffee. Because he didn't limit (or patronize) his readers with his "judgmental interference," an admiring Henry James preferred him to Flaubert.* Nowadays, to quote Francine Prose, when readers and publishers demand happy endings and "sympathetic" characters, "few novelists would have the nerve" to produce Balzac's brand of unsparing, courageous fiction in which the faces of Paris blend corruption, misery, vanity, and glory.† The dying Cousin Bette "kept the secret of her hate" from the family she'd tried to destroy and who, in their ignorance, mourned her "as the angel of the family." When Bette's cousin asks what is the cause of the deep-rooted evil in the world, Balzac's answer is a want of religion and the "encroachment of money . . . another name for egoism solidified. Money has become the measure of everything."

On days when schoolchildren visit the cottage museum—to see Balzac's desk and religious paintings—the garden remains a quiet preserve. Off to the northeast, looming over the Seine, is the landmark Balzac never set eyes on, the Eiffel Tower, opened in 1889. In winter, it's lit at sunset, a twinkling, roaming golden beacon as if in praise of the evening sky.

Nearby

ALLÉE DES CYGNES   *En route to* **Passy,** *get off the elevated and scenic number 6 métro at* **Bir-Hakeim** *(named for a French*

* Peter Brooks, *Henry James Goes to Paris.*
† Honoré de Balzac, *Cousin Bette.* From the introduction by Francine Prose.

victory in North Africa in *1942*), *walk halfway across the lower level of the double métro and road bridge, until you reach the stairway on the left that leads down to this quiet, mesmerizing walk across a narrow man-made island in the Seine lined with plane trees and benches from which you can look up at the exquisite gray grillwork on the top level of the bridge and the sculpted green river gods on the bottom. This was a favorite walk of Samuel Beckett. Returning to the bridge, continue across to the Passy métro station.*

TROCADÉRO GARDENS   *The number 6 métro continues from Passy to* **Trocadéro** *(or you can walk). By some accounts Trocadéro is a monumentally ugly stone heap facing the Eiffel Tower, and by others it is "the prettiest spot in Paris. The hill of Chaillot— the historic name of the place . . . this view over the Seine, just where the river swings south-westwards, is unequaled by any other."* [*] *The gardens, with jet fountains, pine trees, flowers, and meticulously groomed hedges, slope down to the Seine, and at sunset the dome of* **Les Invalides** *in the distance glows like liquid gold. It's a friendly public space where people—and their strollers, skateboards, and scooters—have a good time. Atget photographed these sprawling gardens before the present* **Place du Trocadéro** *was built in 1937. A bronze sculpture of Benjamin Franklin, Passy resident, at the end of rue* **Benjamin Franklin** *injects a kindly American presence on the Place. Ambassador Franklin was happy in Paris: he was "among a people that love me, and whom I love."* Stacy Schiff's *dazzling* A Great Improvisation: Franklin, France, and the Birth of America *would make the perfect literary companion for a visit to the Trocadéro Gardens.*

---

[*] Gregor Dallas, *Métro Stop Paris.*

THE RIGHT BANK

Nymph, in the Jardin des Tuileries

JARDIN DES TUILERIES

ENTRANCES: rue de Rivoli; place de la Concorde; the
  Louvre; the Solferino footbridge from Musée d'Orsay
MÉTRO: Tuileries; Concorde; Palais-Royal
HOURS: daily, 7:30–7

Whether you walk west to east or east to west—the preferable route, along the "grand axis" in the direction of the obelisk in *Place de la Concorde*, the *Champs-Élysées*, and the *Arc de Triomphe*—the garden of the *Tuileries* of central Paris has survived a history of violence such as you would never imagine from the perspective of today's fastidiously groomed flower beds and treescapes.

Once the private preserve of royal families, the garden displays a dazzling formal design decorated with gleaming white sculptures of mythological and historical celebrities. You can spend hours here, people-watching from a bench next to the lovely statue *Nymph*, promenading along the many graveled paths, thinking back to, say, Henry IV, who walked here, edgy with premonition, the night before he was murdered, or Marie Antoinette, who also strolled anxiously after 1789 when she was imprisoned in the Tuileries palace: one night she escaped, only to get lost in in the unmapped city she'd never set foot in on her own.*

The more than one thousand trees—linden, sycamore, pine, palm, maple, clipped horse chestnut, boxed orange—provide

---

*Graham Robb, *Parisians*: *An Adventure History of Paris*.

ample shade and breezes. The basins are ringed with chairs. You can watch the children navigating boats with long poles, or, alongside the northern terrace—*La Terrasse des Feuillants*—delighting in the trampoline facing the statue of the brilliant author of fairy tales *Charles Perrault* (1628–1703), his Puss 'n Boots character tucked in to his side. Bright flowers decorate the lawns, a sweeping green, luminous under the wide spray of fountains. Cafés, inside the deep greenery of chestnut groves, offer shade and decent food; the café on *La Terrasse de Pomone* faces a pool of water lilies with a statue of Daphne pursued by Apollo; in the southwestern corner of the "riverside" terrace overlooking the Seine (where the imprisoned Marie Antoinette and the dauphin used to walk), the *Orangerie* displays *Monet*'s *Water Lilies*, a kind of homage to the beauty of the city and of the world (daily, except Tues, 12:30–7; Fri, 12:30–9).

Originally owned and occupied by the city's tile manufacturers in the thirteenth century, the site of the tile works—*tuileries* in French—was bought by François I in 1517. It was his daughter-in-law, Catherine de Medicis, who, as the grieving widow of Henri II, claimed the property for herself. The niece of a pope and daughter of a Florentine banker, Catherine loved elaborate gardens in the style of the Italian Renaissance popular in sixteenth-century Florence. Although the *Tuileries Garden* has since known many different configurations—*André Le Nôtre* (1633–1700), the great landscape artist, designed both *Versailles* and the *Tuileries* we see today—it was a grieving Medici queen mother who first established the lavish garden, with a palace thrown in on the side, in the heart of the capital. Paris disliked her extravagance: Ronsard (1524–1585), the "prince of poets," put it this way:

The queen must cease building; Her lime must stop swallowing our wealth. . . . Of what use is her Tuileries to us? Of none, Moreau: it is but vanity.[*]

Like Catherine herself, the Tuileries' history during her reign as queen dowager was tempestuous. Strolling under the lindens one August afternoon in 1572, the fanatically Catholic Catherine is reputed to have discussed, planned, and given the signal for the Saint Bartholomew's Day Massacre on August 24. With her approval, fifteen thousand Protestants were slaughtered in a frenzy of religious hatred, their bodies hacked to death around the **Louvre,** the **Tuileries,** and the French countryside. Catherine's pathetic son, King Charles IX, looked on from his window in the Louvre: "Kill them all! Kill them all!" he cried.[†] In Rome, the triumphant pope ordered a *Te Deum* sung. Two centuries later, during the Terror, the garden witnessed the massacre of the Tuileries palace's Swiss Guards. In 1871, the Paris Commune burned the palace to the ground: it was never rebuilt. But the garden, the oldest and largest public green space in Paris, has survived for almost five centuries.

Just inside the entrance at **Place de la Concorde**—"one of the true wonders of the world," in the words of Ina Caro's *Paris to the Past*—to the left of the large octagonal basin, the statue of **Le Silence** stands out from the crowd, as if coolly contemplating the passage of time. A sensual and graceful figure, her dispassionate gaze registers the garden's mortal haunted beauty, its bloody history buried under the linden trees.

[*] Robert J. Knecht, *The French Renaissance Court.*
[†] Ibid.

These days, there's no anguish here, no fights, no arguments, no noise. The crowds of spring and summer are full of smiles and kissing couples; no one seems in a hurry. You can imagine Edith Wharton and her lover, Morton Fullerton, who in the early twentieth century sat on a terrace above the Seine, long after Marie Antoinette walked in the same spot, under the same trees. "He said 'My love! My darling!' How happy I was!'" Wharton later wrote. "Never had we been happier. . . . Blissful hours."*

Nearby

GALIGNANI   *224, rue de Rivoli. The Galignani family, which began publishing in 1520 in Italy, is now the legendary owner of the first English-language bookshop established on the continent, in business at this location since 1856. A fine interior of dark wood paneling shelves fiction, politics, art history, travel, and many titles published in America and England and translated into French.*

ANGELINA'S   *Next to Galignani, at 226, rue de Rivoli. The crowded tea room, beloved of Parisians and travelers for its* chocolat chaud *and Mont Blanc, faces the* Tuileries *through the arches of rue de Rivoli.*

CHURCH OF SAINT-GERMAIN L'AUXERROIS   *Walk east through the* Tuileries, *past the* **Louvre** *and its oldest part, the beautiful* **Cour Carrée.** *Cross rue de l'Amiral de Coligny and place du Louvre and a median of tulips and trees to enter the front porch of what used to be the parish church of the royal families, built on the site of a Viking stronghold. From the belfry of Saint-Germain,*

---

* Hermione Lee, *Edith Wharton.*

the church bell—"la Marie"—rang out the signal to launch the Saint Bartholomew's Day Massacre. These days its Wednesday carillon concert (1:30–2) plays Bach, Couperin, Mozart. Inside, the statue of **Saint Mary of Egypt** *stands in the rear of the lovely thirteenth-century Chapel of the Holy Sacrament, where the medallions in the stained-glass windows bear motifs from the Hebrew Bible: beautiful Esther in the first window; fearless Judith in the second, holding a sword and draped in turquoise, coral, and purple; a brilliant Deborah in the third.*

In the Garden of the Palais-Royal

PALAIS-ROYAL

ENTRANCES: rue de Beaujolais; place du Palais-Royal;
place Colette
MÉTRO: Palais-Royal; Louvre
HOURS: daily, 7:30–8:30

A self-described "migrant" in Paris, who moved many times through many different *quartiers*, **Colette** (1873–1954), France's greatest natural writer according to many critics, finally found her earthly paradise living above the garden of the **Palais-Royal**. In *Places*, she remembers this masterpiece of landscape and architecture, for centuries the social center of Paris and "a unique point on the globe. Visit London, Amsterdam, Madrid or Vienna, you will see nothing like it. . . . It is called the capital of Paris. Everything is to be found there."*

Colette makes you feel her delight as she looks down over the clipped lime trees at dawn and sunset, and, after rain, smelling the fragrance of flowers "that last into late autumn" under the "great ceiling of the Parisian sky." She could see "the tree trunks of the arbor, the quivering of whipped-up water in the great fountain."† The "enchantment" of this place is intensified by the "mutual courtesy" of her neighbors, who included her friend Jean Cocteau. During the Occupation (1940–1944), when the Nazis made daily raids through the *Palais* apartments, hunting for Jews, Colette's neighbors

---

* Louis Sebastien Mercier, *Tableau de Paris.*
† Colette, *Places.*

hid her Jewish husband, Maurice Goudeket, in their tiny maids' rooms and crawl spaces, saving him from deportation. She, in turn, learning that some of her neighbors, like most of Paris, were hungry during the war, gave them food and money.

Characteristically, there's not a hint of puritanism in the free-spirited Colette's approach to the history of the *Palais-Royal* (originally *Palais-Cardinal*, as the site of the palace Cardinal Richelieu built for himself). She mentions its "bad" reputation, then summons the ghosts of the "ladies of pleasure" who once, like her, must have enjoyed the view of the garden beneath their windows. Historians detail the lineage of the *Palais-Royal* as "the home of Parisian hedonism." In addition to the wild commerce of brothels, gambling houses, and taverns inside the colonnades, both before and after 1789, the coffeehouses welcomed journalists and politicians, bourgeoisie and aristocrats, who argued the radical politics that led to the Revolution.

> *The storming of the Bastille on 14 July 1789 . . . had its origins in the Palais-Royal. It was there, legend has it, that the journalist Camille Desmoulins stood on a café table to . . . launch a call to arms. . . . As Victor Hugo later put it, it was "the core of the comet Revolution."**

Today the *Palais-Royal* is a refuge of tranquillity, beautiful in all seasons but especially in spring. A profusion of yellow and white tulips frame a pretty fountain surrounded by magnolia and lime trees and Parisians on benches reading and sleeping and taking the sun. (Colette often observed from

---

* Colin Jones, *Paris: The Biography of a City.*

her window how devoted Parisians are to books.) There's little traffic into the shops of the arcades. At the north end, where Colette lived (there's a plaque on *9, rue du Beaujolais*), one of her (and Julia Child's) favorite restaurants, **Grand Véfour** (17, rue du Beaujolais, under the northwestern arcades), opened in the 1780s as the Café de Chartres, and still serves its haute cuisine in an elegant dining room. The *Muscade,* a friendly modest café just south of it, with outdoor tables, serves a "salade Colette."

On the occasion of Colette's death, though the nearby church of Saint-Roch refused her a Catholic funeral Mass, she received the first state funeral that France ever gave a woman. Her bier rested in the **Palais-Royal**'s *Cour d'Honneur* in front of Cardinal Richelieu's original palace. Thousands of Parisians, mostly women, filed past, leaving bunches of wildflowers in her honor.*

Nearby

COMÉDIE FRANÇAISE THÉÂTRE (LA MAISON DE MOLIÈRE) *Located in the southwest corner of place Colette, an entrance to the garden of the Palais-Royal.*

CAFÉ NEMOURS   *A brass-fronted hangout of theater people, across from the baubly and aluminum métro entrance on place Colette.*

LIBRAIRIE DELAMAIN, PLACE DU PALAIS-ROYAL   *Cross place Colette and walk south. The bookstore stocks Colette's writing, in French. On its walls are photographs of French writers Annie Ernaux, Marguerite Duras, Marguerite Yourcenar, as well*

---

* Judith Thurman, *Secrets of the Flesh: A Life of Colette.*

as foreigners Henry James, Samuel Beckett, Edith Wharton, and Djuna Barnes.

CHURCH OF NOTRE-DAME DES VICTOIRES   *Place des Petits-Pères. Through the north end of the Palais-Royal at rue de Beaujolais—detouring through the elegant covered passage of* **Galérie Vivienne,** *home to a good antiquarian bookstore,* **Librairie Jousseaume**—*you come to this friendly little square where boys play soccer in front of Colette's parish church. A baptized Catholic and lifelong agnostic, she lit candles here before a Marian altar (still ablaze with the vigil lights of Parisians) for her friends who were sick and in danger during the Occupation.*

CHURCH OF SAINT-ROCH   *West, on rue Saint-Honoré.* **André Le Nôtre** *(1613–1700), the landscape designer of Versailles and the Tuileries, had his workshop in Saint-Roch. Behind the* **Wall of the Deportation** *are buried pieces of earth from ten German concentration camps as well as the ashes of French deportees.*

The descent into the Vallée Suisse

LA VALLÉE SUISSE

ENTRANCE: the corner of avenue Franklin D. Roosevelt
and Cours la Reine
MÉTRO: Invalides; Franklin D. Roosevelt
HOURS: daily, 24 hours

One of my favorite places in Paris.
—ELAINE SCIOLINO*

Thanks to Sciolino, the former correspondent for the Paris bureau of *The New York Times*, who wrote about her adopted city's out-of-the-way green spaces, you can find your way to the **Swiss Valley**. It's easy to miss.

Immediately to the right of a melodramatic sculpture of romantic poet Alfred Musset—his "male gaze" resting upon an assortment of his swooning naked lovers and muses (George Sand, the best known)—some narrow, cracked stone stairs lead down into the hidden "valley." What you find at the bottom comes as a surprise and delight: utter quiet and simple beauty to the accompaniment of the sound of water flowing from a small waterfall into a pond shaped by rocks and shaded by an old weeping beech tree. There's a surround of tall evergreens and maples rising toward the sky, bushes thick with lilacs and jasmine, roses in bloom in late October. The wooden footbridge has the look of a set design. (Sciolino describes the place, aptly, as "a tiny stage-set.") It's an enchanting and comforting place, a sanctuary that's part of the

---

*Elaine Sciolino, "Hidden Gardens of Paris," *The New York Times*.

larger and more public *Champs-Élysées* gardens where you can be completely alone—or not—in the middle of a great metropolis.

Returning to the street above, you encounter some humor on the corner of the intersection of avenue Franklin Roosevelt and Cours la Reine: the sternly heroic sculptures of Jacques Cartier and Samuel Champlain, seventeenth-century explorers in the New World, who appear just next to the swoony lyricism of the nineteenth-century Musset tableau.

Nearby

PETIT PALAIS, THE INTERIOR GARDEN   *Avenue Winston Churchill; open daily except Mon, 10–6. The most dramatic approach is from the Left Bank, across the* **Pont Alexandre III,** *the most extravagant of the Seine bridges, named to please Russia in 1900 at a time of expanding German domination. The* **Petit Palais,** *on the right, has a pretty interior garden and indoor-outdoor café. The outdoor tables face the wonderful dome of the* **palais** *and a garden dense with palm and banana trees and pools decorated with gold and blue mosaics. The design of the tile floor of the main lobby is another among many highlights of this delightful free museum, which also offers concerts and lectures about Parisian culture. Ask at the information desk.*

PALAIS DE LA DÉCOUVERTE IN THE GRAND PALAIS   *Avenue Franklin D. Roosevelt; open Tues–Sun, 9:30–6. An interactive science museum beloved by Parisian schoolchildren.*

GARDENS OF THE CHAMPS-ÉLYSÉES   *Walk west from the* Place de la Concorde, *called "the Heart of Paris," along avenue Gabriel under a canopy of sycamores, plane trees, pines, magnolias, chestnut trees, with bleeding hearts still blooming in November. The*

Élysées *palace is to your right, protected—and inaccessible—by high hedges. At the circle—***Rond Point des Champs-Élysées—** *there's a taxi stand. Or you can take the long walk along opulent* **avenue Montaigne** *to* **11, avenue du President Wilson,** *where you'll find the* **Museum of Modern Art of the City of Paris,** *located in one of the two wings of the* **Palais de Tokyo.** *The permanent exhibits—especially Dufy's* La Fée Électricité (The Good Fairy Electricity), *at 250 panels the largest painting in the world—are superb (Matisse, Picasso, Chagall). There's a spacious terrace with palm trees and café service, overlooking the Seine through a screen of plane trees.*

Place des Vosges, southwest corner

The Marais

PLACE DES VOSGES

ENTRANCES: rue Saint-Antoine and rue de Birague,
   through the southern Pavillon du Roi (King's
   Pavilion); through the northern Pavillon de la Reine
   (Queen's Pavilion); east of rue de Turenne
MÉTRO: Saint-Paul; Bastille; Chemin Vert
HOURS: daily, 24 hours

Paris remembers this open-air square in the heart of the *Marais* as the inspiration of its best-loved king and urban planner, *Henri IV.* The lovely harmony of its proportions—the border of thirty-six mansions of warm red brick and white limestone around the quadrangle, the tall fountains watering each of the four corners, the arches and arcades lining the perimeter, the rows of linden trees bordering the arcades—*Place des Vosges* has a graciousness resonant with the memory of the *Vert Galant.* Long before it became politically correct, Henri IV made religious tolerance the ideal of his reign, and this square, his masterpiece, reflects the sophistication and magnanimity of that ideal.

The site, originally the royal grounds—*Château des Tournelles*—of Henri II, was near the scene of his accidental death in 1559 from wounds received in a jousting tournament on what is now *rue Saint-Antoine.* In mad reaction, his widow, Queen Catherine de Medicis, had *Tournelles* razed, sent Henri II's mistress, Diane de Poitiers, packing, and moved her own entourage west, where she built herself another palace in the *Tuileries.* But a few kings later, in 1605, *Henry of*

Navarre—or *Henri IV*—wanting a new palace and a neigh-borhood free of the Valois dynasty's taint, looked east to the medieval *Marais:* it had been a *quartier* of watered gardens (*maraichers*) rather than an actual marsh. There he began *Place des Vosges* (originally called *Place Royale*) but didn't survive to savor its finished glory. From the outset this enclave ob-served rituals of luxurious pleasure among the resident aris-tocrats: weddings, tournaments (more jousting), balls, fairs, duels, and, the speciality of *le grand siècle*—the great age of the seventeenth century—the *salon,* an elite cultural gather-ing presided over by women.* Effervescent with conversation and political debate as well as news of the amours of Paris, the elegant houses (or hôtels) on the great square entertained the city's most original wits in their salons. Molière, his rival Racine, La Fontaine, La Rochefoucauld, Boileau, *Madame de Sévigné,* who was born at 1 bis, place des Vosges, and her best friend, Madame de Lafayette, all became regulars.

One salon to which the richest and sexiest were most faithful was presided over by *Ninon de l'Enclos* (1620–1705). Like all Frenchwomen of the seventeenth century, Ninon in her youth had had four vocational choices: wife, nun, prosti-tute, or governness. Her career as a nun fell to ground after a year in the convent. Returning home—to 36, rue des Tour-nelles just off the northeast corner of *Place des Vosges*—she settled in to host what became a fabled literary salon. And as a fabled courtesan (she was determined not to marry), she entertained many lovers, famous nobles as well as the priests and bishops who denounced her from the Sunday pulpit, ob-

---

* Stacy Schiff, *A Great Improvisation: Franklin, France, and the Birth of America.* "The women of France . . . kept the salon, which was the equivalent of run-ning the newspapers."

jecting more to the woman (and author, in her private hours) who scorned organized religion than to Ninon the courtesan. Molière wrote that "she has the keenest sense of the absurd of anyone I know." His *Les Précieuses Ridicules* (*The Pretentious Young Ladies*) mocked the idle chitchat of the salons and their *salonnards* (sycophants). The pious Queen Anne of Austria, mother of King Louis XIV, had Ninon locked up in jail for a few months—actually, a convent—more for her influence than her transgressive sexual mores. "Feminine virtue is nothing but a convenient masculine invention," Ninon observed. Her guests listened to her unconventional *bon mots*, including the memoirist Saint-Simon, who took notes. When Ninon died, she left money to Voltaire, whom she'd met when he was a nine-year-old boy, to buy books.

On late Sunday afternoons in all seasons, Parisian families gather and stroll in *Place des Vosges,* in summer finding shade under the trees that surround the statue of Louis XIII, the son of *Henri IV.* Dusk moves in and the cafés under the arcades fill up. On weekday mornings, the square is almost empty, except for the twittering swallows. It's a lovely place to sit and read Madame de Lafayette's *La Princesse de Clèves* (1678), the first significant French novel, its subject the adulterous passion of a young Frenchwoman for another man, set in the court of King Henry II, at *Tournelles,* before and after his fatal jousting. Or for less serious history, the 1,500 letters of *Madame de Sévigné* take you back to the heyday of the gossipy and promiscuous salons (both her husband and son were lovers of Ninon) when the intelligentsia and artists of Paris first looked out over the magical square. Its founding *bon vivant* would have adored it.

Nearby

PARIS WALKS   *For more facts and fiction while walking through this legendary* quartier: *33.1.48.09.21.40, www. paris-walks.com.*

JARDIN SAINT-GILLES GRAND VENEUR   *Via rue des Arque-busiers or rue Villehardouin, through an archway, a two-minute walk from Place des Vosges, to the northeast. In spring and summer, this secret garden is framed by trellises of roses against a background of elegant tall apartments. The crowds of travelers afoot in the Marais are within neither sight nor sound. There is a plaque in honor of Pauline Roland (1805–1852), socialist, teacher, and feminist, who was imprisoned in Algeria for resisting Napoleon III's coup d'état in 1851.*

HÔTEL SULLY   *The main entrance is at 2, rue Saint-Antoine. The mansion, the residence of Henri IV's finance minister, the duc de Sully, has a pretty garden, with benches and orange trees and no sound of the traffic on Saint-Antoine. In the southwest corner is an excellent bookstore*—**Librairie des Monuments Historiques**—*well-stocked with books about Paris (for example,* Le Monde de Colette au Palais-Royal*). Open Tues–Sun. Through an archway in the northeast corner is another entrance to* **Place des Vosges.**

PLACE DU MARCHÉ SAINTE-CATHERINE   *Walking west along rue Saint-Antoine, almost opposite the Church of Saint-Louis–Saint-Paul, turn right into rue Caron, which leads straight into this small neighborhood square facing rue d'Ormesson. Nice bistros and benches, under the trees.*

Jardin de Musée Carnavalet

JARDIN DE MUSÉE CARNAVALET

ENTRANCES: 23, rue de Sévigné; 16, rue des Francs-
Bourgeois
MÉTRO:S aint-Paul
HOURS: Tues–Sun, 10–5:30.

Once inside the courtyard of *Carnavalet* you're sur-rounded by one of the most formidable historic build-ings in the *Marais. Hôtel Carnavelet* (now a museum), built in 1546 under the influence of the Italian Renaissance, over-looks the highly formal and symmetrical design of the small French garden. The mansion has two wings at right angles to it. The four reliefs on the main façade opposite the entrance—*The Seasons*—are the work of the Renaissance sculptor Jean Goujon (1510–1564), admired by Bernini, who also carved the decorations on the southwest side of the *Cour Carrée*—the "square courtyard" part of the Louvre palace—and on the façade of the *salle*—the reception room—on the ground floor of the Louvre.

The grounds of *Carnavalet* delighted *Madame de Sévigné* (1626–1696), one of the greatest letter writers in French lit-erature, who lived in the hotel for the last twenty years of her life and wrote many of her letters here, outdoors, in the shadow of her residence.* "It is an admirable affair, we shall all stay here and enjoy the fine air. Since it is impossible to have everything, we shall have to dispense with parquet floors

---

*Madame de Sévigné, *Selected Letters*, trans. Leonard Tancock.

and fashionable little stoves; but at least we have a fine court-yard, a beautiful garden, and nice little blue girls who are most convenient." (The "blue girls" were nuns who lived in a convent in *rue Sévigné*—then called rue Sainte-Catherine—where the Lycée Victor-Hugo now stands. They wore a blue habit.)*

Madame de Sévigné's correspondence has, for more than three centuries, received high praise for its range as well as its style, an unusual mix of elegant and natural. An educated woman, widely read in history, philosophy, religion, and theology as well as the French moralists Montaigne, Rabelais, and her contemporaries Corneille, Molière, La Fontaine, and Pascal, she wrote to friends and family about the intrigues and comedy of *le grand siècle*, Paris under Louis XIV. But her main subject was her obsessive love for her married daughter, who lived in Provence, that distance the cause of her mother's mournful and repetitious confessions of love and longing. Because she grew up in the Marais as an orphan—her parents were dead by the time she was seven—one Madame de Sévigné biographer believes these childhood losses fueled her morbid attachment to her own maternity.† Another of her pet subjects was health, protecting it, defending oneself against inevitable hateful death as well as the horror of getting fat. A regular at the spa at Vichy where she purged and sweated, she had strong opinions on the importance of keeping the bowels open—chocolate and coffee are recommended; of getting enough sleep; of not getting pregnant too often. Although Saint-Simon found her "lovable" and "such excellent company," to her daughter's husband, the opinionated Madame de

---

* Eric Hazan, *The Invention of Paris: A History in Footsteps*.

† Francine du Plessix Gray, "Mother Love: Madame de Sévigné," in *Adam and Eve in the City: Selected Nonfiction*.

Sévigné, who also offered contraceptive advice, was a mother-in-law from hell. A practicing Catholic, she worshipped close to home, at *Saint-Paul–Saint-Louis,* 99, rue Saint-Antoine, a Jesuit church modeled on the Gesu in Rome.

The interior of *Musée Carnavalet* and the adjoining *Hôtel le Peletier de Fargeau* offer excellent exhibits about the history of Paris. Madame de Sévigné's apartments are reconstructed on the first floor, in room 21, with her writing desk as well as portraits of her and her literary friends. After her death, her uptight descendents sugarcoated some of her letters before their publication, just as the prissy English daughter of Lady Mary Wortley Montagu would "edit" her mother's brilliant *Embassy Letters* (1763), a correspondence Voltaire rated superior to Madame de Sévigné's.

Nearby

LA TARTINE   *rue du Roi de Sicile (rear entrance) or 24, rue de Rivoli. A good old (1900) café with political associations—the* Politburo *met here—in this once radical neighborhood of artisans and workers. Rue du Roi de Sicile figures in a first-rate novel set in pregentrification* Marais *during the Algerian War,* The Mark of the Angel *by Nancy Huston (1999).*

QUARTIER SAINT-PAUL–SAINT-GERVAIS   *South of Musée Carnavalet. The quiet empty streets and hidden gardens between rue Saint-Antoine and rue de Rivoli and the Seine offer much to enjoy:* **rue des Barres, rue Pont Louis Philippe, rue François-Miron,** *the* **Maison Européenne de la Photographie,** *rue de Fourcy, Mon–Tues, 5–7; Wed–Sun, 11–8; www.mep-fr.org). The public library,* **Bibliothèque Forney** *in Hôtel de Sens, has a charming garden, at 1, rue du Figuier, métro, Pont-Marie; Tues–Fri, 1:30–8:30.*

Square Georges-Cain

SQUARE GEORGES-CAIN

ENTRANCE: 8, rue Payenne

MÉTRO: Saint-Paul; Chemin Vert

HOURS: Mon–Fri, winter, 7:30–5:30; summer, 7:30–9:30;
weekends, open 9:00

A pretty square, as well as an archaeological depository of stone fragments from older gardens like the *Tuileries.* The benches, which face a circular central garden with a bronze sculpture called *Dawn,* seem the most favored preserve of Parisians reading *Le Monde* or basking in silence under a pale sun. In late spring you're surrounded on all sides by a profusion of blooming rosebushes. The square, which opened in 1931, is bordered on its east side by the back of the *Carnavalet* museum in *rue de Sévigné* where *Georges Cain* (1856–1919), a painter and writer, was the first curator. Extending along the square's north perimeter is the seventeenth-century *Orangerie* of the *Hôtel le Peletier de Saint-Fargeau,* the mansion at a right angle to *Carnavalet.* Both mansions are linked together by a long gallery. Wrapped in the hush and privacy of this square, you'd never guess you're only minutes away from the crowded heart of Marais museum country: *Musée Picasso, Musée d'Art et d'Histoire du Judaisme,* the *Archives Nationales de France, Musée de l'Histoire de France,* and *Musée Cognacq-Jay,* each a short walk to the west. *Square Georges-Cain* is truly the Paris that keeps to herself.

Nearby

SQUARE LÉOPOLD-ACHILLE   *At the north corner of rue Payenne as it ends in rue du Parc Royal. A large lawn crowded with reclining families on Sunday afternoons, who can look up at the magnificent mansions along rue du Parc Royal. Francis I raised camels and ostriches in the large Parc Royal, which gave its name to the street. Outside the railings boys play football, in front of Café Sévigné. East of the lawn is a playground.*

CAFÉ DES MUSÉES   *At the corner of rue du Parc Royal and 49, rue de Turenne. A very good bistro with an upstairs and downstairs dining room, the food and ambience especially satisfying on cold nights in fall and winter. Open daily. No reservations.*

CLOS DES BLANCS-MANTEAUX   *21, rue des Blancs-Manteaux, the street Sartre wrote a song about. This small enclosed garden of* biodiversité *has a modest charm, with 250 varieties of plants, dedicated to the memory of Princess Diana, who died in Paris on August 31, 1997. It's only open on weekends. During the week there's a day-care center and preschool in the surrounding buildings.*

Square du Temple, in the northern Marais

SQUARE DU TEMPLE

ENTRANCES: rue du Temple; rue de Bretagne; rue
   Perrée; rue Eugène-Spuller
MÉTRO: Temple; Arts et Métiers
HOURS: dawn to dusk, according to the season

On a quiet Sunday morning—the sleepy fathers mind-ing toddlers and solitaries sitting under the apple trees, deep in newspapers—it would never cross your mind that *Square du Temple* has been eyewitness to carnage, confla-gration, torture, regicide, genocide, eight centuries of atroc-ities buried alive in Parisian memory.

In 1140, the site became the headquarters of the Knights Templar, a hugely wealthy and propertied international re-ligious order established to protect pilgrims to Jerusalem. The Templars' territory included large swaths of land in the northern and southern *Marais*. Their fortress, a tower-ing castle, was inhabited by thousands of monk-soldiers; in the center of the enclosure was the prison. The Tem-plars acted as bankers to financially stressed kings, hiding them on occasion from rioting mobs. In 1307, in need of cash, the savage *Philippe le Bel* (he was good-looking) de-clared war on the Templars. Charging them with heresy, sodomy, and necromancy, he invaded, razed, arrested, tor-tured, and burned at the stake the monks who would not confess, including *Jacques Molay*, the Father General: he was hung from the scaffold and burned alive, near the Square

Vert Galant. Louis XVI, Marie-Antoinette, and the dauphin (Louis XVII) and his sister were imprisoned in the same Temple keep where the Templars had been tortured, before the king and queen went to the guillotine in 1793; the dauphin was held for another three years, when he died. Napoleon, afraid the site would become a destination of royalist pilgrims, had the prison razed.

Today there's a large sign in the square bearing the names of the youngest children—unrecorded in school registers—who were deported by the Nazis from the *Marais* homes bordering the square, once the property of the incinerated Templars, later the neighborhood of Jewish artisans and merchants.

At the *rue de Bretagne* entrance there's a lovely rock garden and pond with a small waterfall, another triumph of the engineer and landscape architect *John-Charles Adolphe Alphand.* All along the paths the gardens are planted with spirea and lilacs and flowering fruit trees. Near the western edge, you pass the sculpted head of the poet and songwriter *Béranger,* the French Robert Burns, whose socialist sympathies and lyrics landed him in jail in the nineteenth century. Winding back toward the bandstand, where there are concerts in spring and summer, you pass a bird sanctuary, dense with shrubbery and trees, the birds performing like divas in the Sunday air.

Nearby

MARCHÉ DES ENFANTS-ROUGES   *The oldest covered food market in Paris, named for an orphanage founded on this site by Francis I: the orphans wore red. The narrow entrance is off rue de Bretagne and rue Charlot. (Tues–Sat, 8:30–1, 4–7:30; Sun, 8:30–2). Inside, a lively and diverse clientele order food to suit many ethnic tastes.*

MUSÉE DES ARTS ET MÉTIERS   *A short walk, at 60, rue de Reaumur; Tues–Sun, 10–6; Thurs, until 9:30. It is part of the Conservatoire des Arts et Métiers, with a wide range of exhibits and information about technological innovation. On its south side, on the ancient rue Saint-Martin (passing Saint-Martin des Champs and Saint-Nicholas des Champs), you will find the small* **Square E. Chautemps,** *under chestnut trees; a Wallace fountain—a symbol of Parisian parks and squares—faces the* Conservatoire.

AU-DELÀ DES FRONTIÈRES   *A short walk east, across boulevard Filles du Calvaire, at 106, rue Amelot. A good fair-trade shop with handmade toys, jewelry, and artifacts made in Africa and Asia, a jewel of the laid-back eleventh* arrondissement.

LE CENTENAIRE   *104, rue Amelot, at the corner of rue Oberkampf; métro, Filles du Calvaire. A high-spirited neighborhood bistro. Open 7–midnight; closed Sunday night.*

IL PREZZEMOLO OSTERIA ITALIANA   *13, rue Commines; métro, Filles du Calvaire. Open every day: a good choice on Sunday nights when many* Marais *bistros and restaurants are closed.*

HÔTEL BEAUMARCHAIS   *3, rue Oberkampf; tel: 01.53.36.86. 86; www.hotelbeaumarchais.com. A friendly, modestly priced hotel, with an outdoor breakfast café, a minute's walk from the métro and boulevard Filles du Calvaire: cross it and you're in the Marais. In the other direction (left as you exit the hotel), you head up the hill of Oberkampf into the eleventh* arrondissement *and "the increasingly energetic northeast quadrant of the city."**

*Mark Bittman, "In Paris, Farther-Flung for Taste and Value," *The New York Times.*

Parc Monceau, northern Paris

PARC MONCEAU

ENTRANCES: boulevard de Courcelles and avenue Hoche;
   avenue Velasquez; avenue Van Dyck; avenue Ruysdael
MÉTRO: Monceau; Courcelles
HOURS: daily, 7–8

No matter which of the wildly ornate gates you enter through, *Parc Monceau* strikes you right off as sign *extraordinaire* of Paris as a culture of elegance. André Maurois finds the context of the city's high-toned character in the "tradition of taste inherited from centuries of cultivation," her "atmosphere of beauty" so radiantly manifest in "the graciousness of her cities." The collective reverence for beauty—the expectation of it—is the offspring of the artists, writers, architects, painters, and artisans, who are, for the most part, residents of Paris.* Wandering through *Monceau,* past the classical colonnade, the oval lake, lily ponds, rock gardens, the statues of Chopin, Musset, and Maupassant set into lovely flower beds and sloping lawns, you feel part of this legacy. In June, the roses and gardenia trees in blossom, the air carries the memory of Manet, Gounod, Debussy, Fauré, Dumas *fils,* and Rostand, who all worked or lived in the *Monceau* neighborhood. Today, the streets and mansions of the eighth *arrondissement* that border the park cast a spell of a certain Parisian past, exclusive, privileged. Marcel Proust (1871–1922), who lived nearby, played here as a child; the park is said not

---

* André Maurois, *A History of France.*

to have changed much since then, more than a century later still showing off Paris on her most refined behavior.

A few facts of origin, however, fit neither this "French" nor "privileged" profile. The land started out as the twelfth-century village of *Monceau*. Joan of Arc made her camp here in the fifteenth century. The park itself was designed as an English garden in the eighteenth century; then it acquired a Scottish gardener; the omnipresent Alphand continued the Anglicization in the nineteenth century.

In fiction, **Monceau** loses its civilized veneer, at times becoming a menacing backdrop. In her novel *Claudine in Paris* (1901), Colette plays with the contradiction between the neighborhood's reputation of good taste and the brutal reality:

> *The green Parc Monceau, with its soft lawns veiled in misty curtains of spray from the sprinkler, attracted me, like something good to eat. There were fewer children there than in the Luxembourg. It was better altogether. But those lawns that are swept like floors! Never mind, the trees enchanted me and the warm dampness I breathed in relaxed me . . . that sound of leaves, how sweet it was!**

But the next moment she spots Luce, her best friend from childhood, strolling through the park. An innocent country girl when she ran away to Paris, Luce is now a kept woman, a prostitute, who lives nearby in opulence and servitude in the **rue de Courcelles.** Revolted by the love of money and the fake respectability that the **Monceau** *quartier* exhales, Colette (Claudine) realizes her old friend is now a spiritual ruin, her luxurious clothes a sad disguise.

* Colette, *Claudine in Paris.*

In the movie *Ne le dit à personne* (*Tell No One*, 2006), an anguished and desperate François Cluzet sits on a bench just inside the wrought-iron and golden Courcelles entrance, next to the children's play area and kiosk, waiting for his wife, who may or may not have been brutally murdered. The denouement of this thriller implicates the powerful class at home in this *quartier*, their politesse masking a ruthless corruption.

Jean-Pierre Melville's masterpiece, *L'armée des ombres* (*Army of Shadows*, 1969), based on his own years in the Resistance and on the novel of the same name by Joseph Kessel, ends with the tragic murder of the *Résistante* Mathilde (Simone Signoret) against the background of the high iron gates of the Courcelles entrance to Parc **Monceau**. The Champs-Élysées and the *quartiers* north of it—**Monceau,** for one—were well known during and after World War II as collaborationist territory, dangerous ground for *Résistants* such as Melville, who, in the movie, was captured by the SS near the **Arc de Triomphe.**

Nearby

MUSÉE JACQUEMART-ANDRÉ   *158, boulevard Haussmann, daily, 10–6; métro, Miromesnil. The collection of this grand mansion includes Italian Renaissance masters and Rembrandt, Tiepolo, Mantegna. The café is, understandably, a Parisian favorite.*

LA SALLE PLEYEL   *252, rue du Faubourg Saint-Honoré; métro, Ternes. One of the most famous and handsome concert halls in the world. The café at intermission is delightful, crowded with the mostly Parisian concertgoers.*

CATHÉDRALE SAINT-ALEXANDRE NEVSKY   *17, rue Daru; Tues, Fri, Sun, 3–5. The Russian Orthodox church in the heart of Paris's Little Russia.*

23, AVENUE DE MESSINE   *Follow rue de Monceau to place de Rio de Janeiro, then turn left into avenue de Messine. In Louis Malle's movie* Belle de Jour, *Catherine Deneuve, who lives here with her husband in well-heeled propriety, walks from this address to her secret afternoon job at a nearby brothel.* *

---

*Michael Schurmann, *Paris Movie Walks.*

Musée de la Vie Romantique, the garden a
beloved haunt of Chopin and George Sand

MUSÉE DE LA VIE ROMANTIQUE

ENTRANCE: 16, rue Chaptal
MÉTRO: Saint-Georges; Blanche; Pigalle
HOURS: Tues–Sun, 10–6

At the top of the lane leading to the house, you see on your right the garden, in the shade of huge old chestnut trees, bordered with bushes of bright flowers. Sometimes there's the sound of quiet conversation among the visitors seated at small tables, enjoying the fare of the café. It's not as loud as the singing of the birds nesting in the magisterial chestnuts. The city feels far away, this hidden corner of the ninth *arrondissement* feels out of time, bringing to mind the less cacophonous era of the people who made this place famous. Sitting here, away from the noise of the streets, you find yourself imagining the nineteenth century, the years 1838–1847, say, when the lovers *Frederic Chopin* and *George Sand* (the pen name of *Aurore Dupin Dudevant*) and their friend *Eugène Delacroix* used to visit their friend and neighbor Ary Scheffer, the painter who lived here and worked in the upstairs studio of this house.

The tranquillity of the scene is only a partial evocation of *la vie romantique*, which this garden and house commemorate. Its natural beauty and calm make the perfect backdrop for the story of happy lovers, one a prolific and bold novelist— Sand wrote about the sexual desires and pleasure of women, denounced marriage as "one of the most barbaric institutions society has engendered"—the other a genius, a "divine" pianist and composer who came from Poland. Sand called Chopin her "angel" and nicknamed him "Chip Chip." His music brought her to ecstasy. Passionately devoted to the woman he knew as lover, friend, mother, muse, nurse, manager, and fellow artist, Chopin called her his *Aurore,* his dawn. Delacroix, often accompanied by his cat who was named Cupid, painted a double portrait of them. But after their mutual disenchantment in 1847, the former lovers moved away from this neighborhood. With the failure of romantic love— the loss of trust, the suspicions and resentments—Sand and Chopin became estranged. Alone, sick, and heartbroken, Chopin died two years later, in 1849. Although this tragic end hardly resonates in Scheffer's garden, the dynamic duo of love and death, joy and pain, that figure in Sand and Chopin's story do correspond to the pattern of its seasons: the heat of summer becoming—inevitably—the ice of winter. Such a radical change in temperature brings to mind the emotionally volatile range of nineteenth-century romanticism embodied in the love affair of the great Slavic musician and the French writer.

Inside the museum are cases of memorabilia, mostly of George Sand and her children. Along with jewelry, drawings, letters, and locks of her hair, there is a cast of Chopin's hand.

Nearby

PLACE SAINT-GEORGES　　*As you leave the métro and come into Place Saint-Georges, you see two gorgeous mansions on either side of the square and its storied old fountain. Both are attended by dense and unmanicured greenery: trees, hedges, flowers. Walk down rue Saint-Georges, turn right into rue Saint-Lazare, then, at the post office, take another right to 80, rue Taitbout. Here is the entrance to* **Square d'Orléans** *(open weekdays). A "bright and music-filled utopia of artists," in the words of Benita Eisler,* where Chopin and Sand lived together from 1842 to 1847, though for the sake of appearance Chopin leased the ground floor of number 9, Sand and her children number 5 near the cobblestoned carriage entrance. Built in 1829, the gracious complex, modeled on the architecture of Regency London, was the residential center of* **La Nouvelle Athènes,** *the expensive district that was home to many romantic artists. Here the lovers entertained Balzac; the singer Pauline Viardot, lover of Turgenev; the Polish poet Adam Mickiewicz; as well as Delacroix, Dumas* fils, *and Heinrich Heine. Today, the courtyard's large fountain, between Chopin and Sand's apartments, waters the magnolia tree of the square's private gardens.*

LE DIT-VIN   *68, rue Blanche. A new and good neighborhood wine bar, with a varied menu of bar food and an imaginative wine list.*

---

*Benita Eisler, *Chopin's Funeral.*

Chestnut tree, Square des Batignolles

SQUARE DES BATIGNOLLES

ENTRANCES: place Charles-Fillion; rue Cardinet
MÉTRO: Brochant
HOURS: weekdays, 8–7; weekends, 9:30

The square is especially appealing in bad weather, "bad" as in light misting rain, low clouds of bright silver-gray. The melancholy of Paris and of this *quartier* is palpable. People sit on benches, a few chatting, others fixed in solitary silence, not an umbrella or a smile in sight. The stately chestnut trees, old beautiful presences, like kings and queens of a world of green, breathe in, breathe out, a generous high ceiling of shelter and shade. Baudelaire made poetry out of his hometown's moody "great gray sky," its "mists and rains." "On the other hand," as Caroline Weber puts it, "the city's mists and rains can clear at the drop of a chapeau."*

A pale sun breaks through. More people saunter in, nannies and strollers cross the charming canal bridge and head for a small playground. (Few tourists make it up to *Batignolles* from the city center; many tourist street maps don't extend north of Parc Monceau.) At each of the square's entrances you find a large plaque—*Deco Flo*—detailing the new (2010) floral décor, the names and colors of the plantings. Their unusually asymmetrical design is intended to create *une bonne promenade* along the winding pathways, past the borders of

---

* Caroline Weber, review of Robert Stevens, *Yvon's Paris* in *The New York Times Book Review*.

salvia, verbena, petunias, dianthus, ageratum, and heliotrope
in pretty shades of plumbago blue, rose, red, and white, each
flower bed backed by tall healthy ferns, grasses, palms. You
pass sculpted ducks and geese (and real ones) in the middle
of two elliptical small lakes, and up a hill—hidden within a
small clearing like an exquisite captive princess—you come
upon an *orangerie* near an overview of the train tracks out of
Gare Saint-Lazare.

Like so many Parisian squares, **Batignolles** has known
many incarnations. Originally the site of a warehouse of
demolition materials when the hamlet of Batignolles was
outside the city limits, it became a public space in 1835—*La
Place de la Promenade*—where village festivals and holidays
were celebrated. After 1860, when the village became part
of the city, Napoleon III, as part of his project to make such
spaces into English-style squares—with grottoes and cascades
and miniature lakes—gave the job of transforming Batignolles to his genius landscape architect, Jean-Charles
Adolphe Alphand. Over the next ten years, Alphand would
redesign—Anglicize—twenty-four gardens and parks in all.
(See *Square du Temple, Parc Montsouris, Parc Monceau, Parc
des Buttes-Chaumont, Bois de Boulogne, Bois de Vincennes,*
and *La Vallée Suisse*.)

Near the grotto, the sculpted bust of nineteenth-century
poet **Léon Dierx** commemorates the associations of this
quartier with the many artists—poets and impressionist
painters—who lived and worked in the surrounding streets
and boulevards. **Manet**, **Courbet**, and **Degas**, well-known
to one another and sometime members of the *groupe des
Batignolles*, painted scenes of café and opera house nightlife; Manet captured the poetry of the new nearby railroad
station in *La Gare Saint-Lazare*. **Mallarmé, Leconte de**

Lisle, and ***Paul Verlaine*** (1844–1896) attended the same literary salons, de Lisle and Verlaine coming to detest each other.

Verlaine, who moved with his parents to the Batignolles village as a child, grew up to be considered the "prince of poets" by his peers and an immoral social outcast by bourgeois society. He took part in the Paris Commune, abandoned his wife and child for the poet ***Arthur Rimbaud,*** did time in prison for attempting to murder same, converted to Catholicism, and killed himself with a steady diet of absinthe and beer. He is buried in the nearby *Batignolles Cemetery,* and a piece of his writing—***Christ en Croix***—is affixed to a wall in the ***Église Sainte-Marie des Batignolles,*** just across the tree-lined **Place du Docteur Felix Lobligeois** (with a Wallace fountain in good working order). A statue of Verlaine—a "ragamuffin angel" and "an inspired derelict"—stands in the Luxembourg, in tribute to his poetry—"grey and sad and cool and deep and unlike anything else in the world"* It would remind you on a moody wet November day of the village *Square des Batignolles.* In the soundless stir of the chestnuts, you hear Verlaine's music, "the silence of eternity."

> *"Il pleure dans mon coeur*
> *Comme il pleut sur la ville. . . ."*

Nearby

SQUARE SAINTE-MARIE DES BATIGNOLLES　*Bordered by some pleasant cafés and bistros, an antique shop, and an excellent*

---

*John Cowper Powys, "Paul Verlaine," in *Suspended Judgments: Essays on Books and Sensations.* www.gutenberg.org/ebooks.

bakery with table service. The church itself, which hosts concerts, has a warm feeling.

LA GIOCONDA   *A friendly Italian restaurant—the large house salad is very good—on the corner of rue Brochant and place Charles Fillion, facing the square.*

Square Suzanne-Buisson, Montmartre

SQUARE SUZANNE-BUISSON

ENTRANCE: from Place Casadesus
MÉTRO: Place de Clichy; Lamarck-Caulaincourt
HOURS: 8–8

The most delightful approach to this corner of beauty on the hill of *Montmartre* is from the west: climb rue Caulaincourt from the *Montmartre Cemetery*, midway up take the stairs to the right onto avenue Junot, then a left into rue Simon Dereure, which ends in the charming *Place-des-Quatre-Frères-Casadesus*. The small steps to the right, through a rock garden, take you up to *Square Suzanne-Buisson*. You can sit and recover from the climb in the company of a few Parisians, pairs of friends or lovers, or grandparents keeping an eye on the children in the playground. Birds twitter and don't fly away, diving in and out of the trees, the wildflowers in the rock garden, circling the small greenhouse and the heights of the white mansions of *Place Casadesus,* home to generations of a family of great musicians. If, as Baudelaire said, all art aspires to the condition of music, then here in this square and its beautiful environs—*Allée des Brouillards* ("Fog Alley") and *Place Dalida*—the art of landscape succeeds as a melodious adagio.

Near the front of the square a statue of *Saint-Denis* holding his severed head overlooks the fountain and mall shaded by plane trees. According to legend, when Denis, the first bishop *of Lutetia,* was decapitated by the Romans, c. 258 AD (the site traditionally believed to be at the foot of the *butte* in rue Yvonne le Tac just east of *Place des Abbesses*), he carried his bloody head up to the spring that until the nineteenth century flowed here, washed it, and then continued north to the site of the *Basilica of Saint-Denis,* where he is buried. The origin of the name "*Montmartre*" is commonly thought to be *Mons Martyrum,* after the story of the martyrdom of Denis and his two companions.

The square is named for a victim of a modern totalitarian regime, **Suzanne Levy Buisson,** born in 1883. At the rue Girardin entrance, a "*Histoire de Paris*" plaque identifies her as a martyr of the Resistance and secretary of the Women's Socialist Party. Arrested and tortured by the Nazis, she revealed nothing about the movement. Deported, she died in Germany, the date of her death not known. So little is known about Suzanne Buisson and the other *Résistantes,* her story and the near anonymity of the plaque's profile inject a dissonance into this hilltop place so filled with light. We stand at the entrance, wanting to know more yet grateful to come upon the memory of two people who, in ancient and modern times, had the courage to resist the ruthless force of empire and fascism, two who were murdered for their courage. Again, a musical analogy comes to mind, the jangling harmonics of, say, the French composer Maurice Ravel (who knew *Montmartre*). In the face of a personal disaster, Ravel once said: "I firmly believe that joy is far more fertile than pain." In this *Montmartre* homage to the memory of **Suzanne Buisson** and **Saint-Denis**—in this pretty corner of Paris—there is in their courage a distinct vibration of joy.

Nearby

MONTMARTRE CEMETERY   *8–6; Sun, opens at 9. Entrance off boulevard de Clichy, at the end of avenue Rachel, where there's a map. Here lie Stendhal, Berlioz, Julie Récamier, Heinrich Heine, and Fragonard, under the linden trees, where Colette used to roam and gather flowers. Visitors include German students looking for the grave of Heine. Truffaut (1932–1984), who grew up in Montmartre, is buried here. A scene in* The 400 Blows *takes place on the bridge over the cemetery that leads up rue Caulaincourt to Square Suzanne-Buisson.*

SQUARE CARPEAUX   *"A people's park, the anti-Luxembourg," according to one local. Descend the long flight of steps upon exiting the métro at Lamarck-Caulaincourt, walk west on* rue Marcadet, *then left, down rue Carpeaux. The square is on the right, with a statue of the sculptor* Jean-Baptiste Carpeaux *(1827–1875) surrounded by tall trees flush with singing birds, flower gardens, beds of shrubbery, a kiosk for local concerts, and a statue of a woman without an arm. A scene from Jean-Pierre Melville's Montmartre film,* Bob le flambeur, *takes place here, with the armless woman distinct in the background as Bob the compassionate crook talks business with a partner on a park bench. There is graffiti on a wall:* "Le peuple n'obtient que ce qu'il prend"—*"The people only get what they take." Montmartre was from the first a neighborhood of workers, artisans, and the poor. It's mythologized now as a paradise of the well-heeled and successful artist—Picasso and company—but parts of it were always the territory of rebels, outsiders, and students who couldn't afford the rents in other parts of Paris.*

SQUARE LÉON-SERPOLLET   *Another people's garden built on terraces, the former sites of artists' ateliers. The pretty entrance is from* rue Cloys *(from* rue Marcadet *go down rue Ruisseau and turn left). Built in memory of the children deported by the Vichy government under the German Occupation, the square opens onto the terraces through a pretty arbor and spreads out as you ascend, next to an elementary school. Exiting on rue Marcadet, walk up another long flight of steps to return to rue Caulaincourt; in* **Place Pecqueur,** *there's a sculpted relief of an emigration scene by Steinlein. Next to the* Place *is a good bookstore,* **L'Attrape-Coeurs,** *with a large children's section in the rear.*

LE CÉPAGE MONTMARTROIS *63, rue Caulaincourt, an attractive café, brasserie, and jazz club, not far from the métro.*

Garden behind the Musée de Montmartre, once a
home to Auguste Renoir and studio to Raoul Dufy

MUSÉE DE MONTMARTRE

ENTRANCE: 12, rue Cortot
MÉTRO: Abbesses
HOURS: Tues–Sun, 10–6

The approach to *rue Cortot* from the métro is an exhilarating and scenic climb up the *Montmartre* hill (*butte*): follow *rue des Abbesses* west, right to rue Tholoze, then right again into curvy *rue Lepic* (the old quarry road where Vincent Van Gogh lived with his brother Theo at number 54 in 1886–1888 and where the only windmills of Montmartre still stand); continue uphill along *rue Norvins*—there's a small garden to the left, at *Cité Internationale des Art,* with flowering cherry blossoms in season and a view over *Place Marcel-Aymé*—until the left downhill turn into *rue des Saules* of the willow trees, and, finally, right into the picturesque *rue Cortot.* The entrance to the garden is through the bookshop of the *Musée de Montmartre.*

The loveliness of the garden's setting—it's next to the museum, a seventeenth-century house first owned by an actor-colleague of Molière's—in spring its borders are thick with tulips, a softening grace under tall old trees. Beyond the lily pond and the rear garden are views of the small backyard gardens of *rue Cortot* and, below them, the *Montmartre* vineyards, parallel to *rue des Saules*—all of it feels like a generous reward for the rigors of the ascent. Sitting in the peaceful garden, you can enjoy the beauty of *Montmartre,* knowing you've escaped the crowds thronging *Place du Tertre* and the steps of *Sacré-Coeur.*

The museum offers sketchy details of the hill's history. In the Middle Ages, the abbesses of *Montmartre* owned huge estates up here. *Henri IV* occupied the original twelfth-century Benedictine Abbey (founded by Louis the Fat) during the Siege of Paris in 1589. His artillery dug in on the top of *Montmartre* as he bombarded the starving city below, which was defended from the Protestant *Henri* by armed monks and priests. "My mistress"—Paris—"is very cruel to me," he complained. Having neither wife nor mistress on hand, he seduced the Abbess Claude and another nun in his convent headquarters, rewarding them later with control of the abbeys of Vernon and *Montmartre*. Today the tiny (restored) church of *Saint-Pierre de Montmartre,* behind Sacré-Coeur, is the last surviving vestige of the great abbey where Henri IV flirted with the Catholic Church.[*]

The museum also has a few remnants of *"Red Montmartre,"*[†] where the Paris Commune began in 1871. There's a bust of the Communards' emblematic heroine, *Louise Michel* (1830–1905), the schoolteacher who inspired the seventy-day resistance to the government's army and fought to claim the city for the people who had nothing. She read Baudelaire in the trenches, directed the construction and defense of the barricades, and led more than ten thousand women to fight with her during the bloody and brutal week—*la semaine sanglante*—of May 1871. Many artists and intellectuals supported the rebels or participated themselves in the civil war, including Courbet, Pissarro, Rimbaud, and Verlaine.

---

[*] Hesketh Pearson, *Henry of Navarre: The King Who Dared.*
[†] Eric Hazan, *The Invention of Paris: A History in Footsteps.*

The *Montmartre* of the nineteenth-century painters—Lautrec, Van Gogh, Renoir, Degas, Utrillo—is also represented. Renoir lived in this house and knew the nearby *moulins*—used as dance halls by workers on weekends—painting the famous *Bal du Moulin de la Galette* in 1876 (now in the *Musée d'Orsay*). Raoul Dufy had his studio in the right wing in 1901.

In Van Gogh's time, the hill was dotted with twenty-five windmills—*moulins*—which were being converted into dance halls and cabarets, a feature at the heart of *Montmartre*'s reputation as a neighborhood of pleasure and adventure. The impressionists, in particular, were inspired by the rural atmosphere and the wide sky over the highest point in Paris. "Here, from the top of Montmartre, circles the wonderful city: Paris lighting its lamps in the smoky dusk, shrugging its shoulders at the moon. The Cathedral, Saint-Sulpice, the Panthéon, are toy buildings far across the Seine."*

Van Gogh, however, saw desolation beneath the gaiety of Montmartre (*Le Moulin de la Galette, Festival à Montmartre, La Butte Montmartre,* the latter two in the Rijksmuseum), a perception shared by some of his literary contemporaries, poets Paul Verlaine and Arthur Rimbaud and novelist Émile Zola. What did inspire Van Gogh was the panoramic prospect from the *butte*: the vast city below, often shrouded in fog and smoke, and the Seine running through it.

Nearby

PARC TURLURE   *A neighborhood hilltop green space of many parts, north of Sacré-Coeur. (Back here you hear nothing of the*

* Allan Temko, *Notre-Dame of Paris.*

hordes and buses in front of it.) The most scenic approach is along the village-like **rue Saint-Vincent** *(at the bottom of rue des Saules) past* **Au Lapin Agile**—*a cabaret-bar favored by Picasso, Modigliani, and Utrillo*—*uphill, past the beautiful intersection with* **rue Mont-Cenis** *framed by tall, elegant, ivy-covered mansions with a long view across northern canyons of steep steps until you wind right into* **rue de la Bonne** *and the entrance to the park. With your back to the cascading artificial waterfall (and Sacré-Coeur), you look out over the high brick mansions of Montmartre on the slopes below. Inside the shade of the arbor court, thick with greenery, there is silence and the fragrance of jasmine, which is everywhere.*

SQUARE LOUISE-MICHEL   *"Institutrice, Heroine de la Commune de Paris." At the bottom of the steep, grassy hill beneath Sacré-Coeur, usually a mob scene, the square is built into a circular staircase. A rich grove of trees*—oranges des osages, *chestnuts*—*surrounds the playground, a jubilant scene of music from the carousel and the camaraderie of children and parents from the surrounding multiethnic neighborhoods.*

SQUARE DES ABBESSES   *Walk west from* Square Louise-Michel *to métro Abbesses. A few steps north of the entrance is the little square with the charming* **Je t'aime Wall**—*written 311 times in 250 languages on an enameled fresco made of 511 tiles. The fragments of color represent the pieces of a broken heart.*

Along La Promenade Plantée

Around Bastille and Northeastern Paris

LA PROMENADE PLANTÉE

ENTRANCE: up a stairway or lift at the intersection of rue
  Ledru-Rollin and avenue Daumesnil, south of the
  Bastille opera house
MÉTRO: Bastille; Ledru-Rollin
HOURS: Mon–Sat, 9–7

My Parisian friends prefer New York City's High Line to their own *Coulée Verte,* the first of the abandoned railroad viaducts transformed in the 1990s into a landscaped walkway above the streets of a big city. The newer High Line is wider than the *Promenade Plantée,* more open to the wind off the Hudson River, the plantings more diverse. Walking the Promenade from *Bastille* to the *Jardin de Reuilly*—a midway point—you have a sense of enclosure, of feeling protected along this lush corridor of flowering cherry trees, spirea, jasmine, quince. A still place, except for the play of shadows and sunlight or the slow movement of walkers, the *Promenade* provides plenty of benches for taking a break and enjoying the views: the small rooftop gardens of the apartments to the north that face the walkway, and the architectural façades to the south. (Cinéphiles may recognize the Promenade as a romantic setting in *Before Sunset.*) Like a secular outdoor cloister walk that goes somewhere—as far as the *Bois de Vincennes* if you stay the three-mile course—the *Promenade* in early evening has a meditative calm. As you pass a solo jogger, or parents pushing a stroller, or couples (Julie Delpy and Ethan Hawke look-alikes), you overhear soft exchanges and laughter floating in the air, which, because of the lush vegetation, can be buggy on a warm summer night. But bugs and all, there's something thrilling about this overview of the streets of northeastern Paris, the home ground of *les classes dangereuses.* So much tumultuous history erupted in these *quartiers* below the old railroad tracks (part of the Paris-Cherbourg line). The political uproars and retreats of the *arrondissements* of northeastern Paris come closer to the actual character of the city—its multiple faces and voices—than the tamed tourist areas to the west. Looking down, you can imagine your own scenarios, the atrocities of poverty and injustice that once made these streets the cradle of revolution. You're also walking above the inevitable urban gentrification—or *boboisation* (*bourgeois bohème*)—the designer cafés and arty boutiques inside the sixty arches of the ***Viaduc des Arts,*** the underbelly of ***Avenue Daumesnil.*** Patrons of these hot spots may not be aware of the uncivil past of the twelfth *arrondissement.*

Nearby

JARDIN DE REUILLY   *An inviting meadow of grass and trees, azalea and rhododendron, midway along the* **Promenade Plantée,** *where, after work, at first sign of spring, the neighborhood takes to the lawns. A popular green space with a strong, warm pulse. Head for the Reuilly métro if you've had enough promenading.*

BISTRO DU PEINTRE   *116, Ledru-Rollin, at the Bastille end of the Promenade, on the corner of rue de Charonne. Named for Alexandre Ledru-Rollin, a nineteenth-century radical leftist law-*

yer who owned property in the area. The café-restaurant hasn't changed since it opened in 1902 to the artists and artisans— carpenters, cabinetmakers, ironworkers, blacksmiths—of the eleventh and twelfth arrondissements. *Entering, what catches your eye first is the triptych of mirrors over the long zinc bar; the incised glass behind it, the woodwork, its swirling carvings, the frescoes and little angels and nymphs in fields of flowers on the stucco ceiling—all of it original. Walter Benjamin noted the effect of glass:*

> Paris is a city of mirrors. The asphalt of its roadways smooth as glass, and at the entrance to all bistros glass partitions. A profusion of windowpanes and mirrors in cafés, so as to make the inside brighter and to give all the tiny nooks and crannies, into which Parisian taverns separate, a pleasing amplitude.*

The small dining rooms, on two floors, serve basic bistro fare; the service is smooth, kind to the stranger.

SQUARE RAOUL NORDLING   *Next to the old* Église Sainte-Marguerite *(métro, Charonne), just off rue Charonne between rue Saint-Bernard and Charrière. A melancholy space dedicated to the memory of Raoul Nordling, the Swedish ambassador who, in 1944, persuaded the German General Choltitz to ignore Hitler's order to blow up Paris. Other gardens along these mazelike back streets of artisans, artists,* boulangeries, *and fine old façades and doorways are the communal* Jardin Nomade Saint-Bernard *(Sat–Sun, 11–7, in spring), at the corner of rue Charles Delescluze and rue Trousseau; and the busy* Square Trousseau *on* rue du Faubourg Saint-Antoine.

* Walter Benjamin, *The Arcades Project.*

PARC DE BERCY   *Métro, Bercy. A newish modern park on the grounds of the old wine warehouses of the Right Bank. On the south terrace, the twenty-one sculptures by Rachid Khimoun,* Les Enfants du Monde, *line either side of the* **Simone de Beauvoir** *footbridge, which crosses the Seine to the* **Bibliothèque Nationale Mitterand** *with its interior garden modeled after a pine grove. Cinéphiles visiting Paris could make Bercy their sole destination and be happy: the* **Cinemathèque Française** *at 51, rue de Bercy, the city's film institute, shows films all day, every day, except Tuesday, from its collection of forty thousand plus films, the largest in the world, on the four screens of its multiplex. There's a museum, with special exhibits—a first-rate one about* **Georges Meliès** *(1861–1938), the father of special effects, ran in spring 2008—a café, bookshop, and film library (www.cinemathèque.fr). Outside, the wide lawns, like most Paris parks, are covered with people on weekends. The children's carousel plays Bach's* **Brandenburg** *concertos. The gardens to the east, dedicated to the assassinated Israeli prime minister Yitzhak Rabin, are beautifully designed and varied— tulips, roses, pansies, an unearthly birch grove, an orangerie, majestic trees, rock gardens, bird sanctuaries. Don't miss the high curving staircases over the roadway at the far eastern end, leading to more gardens.*

Parc Floral in Bois de Vincennes

BOIS DE VINCENNES: PARC FLORAL

ENTRANCES: 283, avenue de Daumesnil; avenue de Paris
at the Vincennes métro
MÉTRO: Château de Vincennes; Porte-Dorée; Porte de
Charenton; buses 46 and 86
HOURS: summer, 9:30–8; winter, 9:30–dusk

*No large modern city has been so fortunate as Paris in keeping its
surrounding woodland . . . In the twelfth century these woods were
as wild as the far Sierras and filled with wolves, bear, and leaping
stags.* *

The ***Bois de Vincennes*** began, like the Bois de Boulogne
to the west, as a royal hunting ground in the twelfth century. The thirteenth-century King (later Saint) Louis IX, as
first judge of the realm, famously met his subjects and heard
their cases under an oak tree in the Vincennes forest: "Seated
on a scarlet blanket, dressed in a simple coat of wool but with
a cap of peacock feathers, [he] delivered decisions without
concern for wealth or social rank."† (The oak tree turns up
in many histories, but few mention the wolves.) The saintly
Louis (canonized in 1297) walked back and forth between
Vincennes—in the southeast of the city—and Paris. In both
places he built a chapel. *La Sainte-Chapelle* on the *Île de la Cité*
remains today, a reliquary shrine of blue and flaming ruby-
colored glass, its relic—the Crown of Thorns—now missing.

*Allan Temko, *Notre-Dame of Paris*.
†André Maurois, *A History of France*.

(Louis had bought it after one of his enthusiastic crusades against the heretics in the East.) The royal chapel he built at *Vincennes* has been under restoration for years.

The main attraction for travelers who don't have time to roam the historic woods in search of Louis's oak (the *Bois de Vincennes* is three times larger than Central Park) is *Parc Floral* (www.parcfloraldeparis.com). It has been called the most beautiful flower garden in Paris. Hundreds of species flourish here: a garden of orchids from early March, a dahlia garden in fall, a garden of water lilies and lotus, a forest of camellias, a vast wavelike display of tulips from April on, fields of irises, azaleas, and rhododendrons in May. It's an enchanting garden, seventy-five acres of color and fragrance, with trees reaching toward the sky. Rilke's pantheistic hymn to "the treetops, like a rising from the dead" rings true. In summer, there are free evening outdoor jazz concerts in the park, close by the lovely *Lac des Minimes,* where you can feed the ducks or dine in the island restaurant. Farther away you can rent boats on *Lac Daumesnil.* The stark pine forests of *Parc Floral,* shot through with flashes of sunlight across the smooth forest floor, are popular with picnickers and families. The breezes are bracing, making clear why *Vincennes* to the east of the city and *Boulogne* to the west are called "the lungs of Paris."

Other attractions are the royal medieval buildings on the grounds of the château—a prison (where the Marquis de Sade dreamed of Petrarch's *Laure*), a castle, a fortress, ramparts, an arsenal of cannon for the defense of Paris—occupied by the Germans during World War II. As they withdrew from the castle in August 1944, they shot twenty-six members of the Resistance and set fire to some of the ancient buildings. As you walk the long and dusty courtyard of the military grounds today, you notice there is nothing growing anywhere, not one blade of grass.

Head for the ***Parc Floral***. Or return to the far end of the ***Promenade Plantée*** and head back, in the footsteps of King Louis,* to the city center.

Nearby

BUDDHIST TEMPLE   *Southwest of Parc Floral, across several roads, on the southern side of Lac Daumesnil near the Porte Dorée métro, there's a Buddhist center, with a Tibetan temple, a pagoda, and a Vietnamese chapel. Open spring and summer only; information: 01.43.41.54.48. Boating on Lac Daumesnil, you think you're in the countryside. There's a café on one of the islands.*

---

*For the full story of Louis IX and his purchase of the Crown of Thorns—from a Venetian pawnbroker—see Ina Caro's "Sainte Chapelle in Paris," in *Paris to the Past.*

Square Maurice-Gardette, in *l'onzième*—
the eleventh—*arrondissement*

SQUARE MAURICE-GARDETTE

ENTRANCES: rue Lacharrière; rue Rochebrune; rue du
   General Guilham; 2, rue du General Blaise
MÉTRO: Saint-Maur; Saint-Ambroise
HOURS: daily, 8–dusk

Paris is criticized sometimes for its "distinctly sinister side," something that "makes you feel the blood that has run in the streets,"[*] as if knowing the complex history of Paris spoils the sweet-dream "City of Light, City of Romance." One ex-pat critic suggests a connection between the metallic sky—"Paris is grayness"—and a residue of humiliation left over from the city's compromises during the German Occupation.[†]

Parisians, however, enjoy a more nuanced range of perception. It's partly a matter of a bred-in-the-bone intimacy with their city's psyche and history. They know firsthand so many local settings of that history. Places inscribe themselves on memory, deepening understanding and affection.

Some Parisians have referred to *Square Maurice-Gardette* in the eleventh *arrondissement* of northeastern Paris—historically, the poorest, the most populated, and the most insurrectionary area of the city—as the loveliest neighborhood park in town. Blood did flow here: the square is built on the former *abattoir of Ménilmontant*; in its surrounding streets—*rue Saint-Maur, avenue Parmentier*—barricades defended

---

[*] Brigid Dorsey and Alicia Drake, in *Paris Was Ours*, ed. Penelope Rowlands.
[†] Ibid.

by Communards, eventually slaughtered in 1871, held piles of corpses; during the Occupation, the Gestapo and the gendarmes were a brutal force in this *quartier.*

Today, it's the Resistance and survival of that force that fertilizes the memory of the neighborhood. On October 20, 2010, for instance, the *mairie* of the eleventh paid homage to **Maurice Gardette** and his twenty-six comrades of the Resistance who were shot at Châteaubriant on October 22, 1941. Local people and politicians crowded into the square to commemorate the sixty-ninth anniversary of the heroism of the square's namesake, Maurice Gardette (1895–1941), a metalworker, born and raised in poverty, who lived with his wife and children in nearby **rue Chemin Vert.** A member of the French Communist Party, elected to the city council, he was arrested for his antifascist activism. On October 22, 1941, he wrote on a plank in the barracks of the prison camp: *"Je meurs courageux, plein de foi revolutionnaire"*—"I die courageously, full of revolutionary faith." The citizens of 2010— among them a few elderly *Résistants*—listened to speeches, sang songs popular during World War II, then marched to *Père-Lachaise,* where the bodies and ashes of Maurice Gardette and the other *Fusillés de Châteaubriant* (including Jean-Pierre Timbaud and seventeen-year-old Guy Moquet) are buried, across from the *Mur des Fédérés.*

Though the eleventh *arrondissement* is now a "happening" area according to many journalists, the neighborhood around the square remains unpretentious. Weekends, local families gather around the square's music kiosk, playground, and Ping-Pong tables, filling the benches, strolling the gravel paths, no doubt taking for granted the over two thousand varieties of plantings, the tall healthy trees—sycamores, magnolias, orange trees, black pine, palms, catalpa, and chestnuts—all a

graceful massive canopy rising above the flower beds of lilies, irises, roses, and asters decorating the grass. Beautifully
placed within this thick and colorful greenery is a bronze
sculpture by Jacques Perrin: *Le Botteleur*, an arresting repre-
sentation of a worker bending over in a field to tie the work of
his hands into bunches.

The memory honored in **Square Maurice-Gardette** in
October 2010 fertilizes the green heart of Paris, saves it from
historical amnesia. (As Milan Kundera has said, "The struggle against power is the struggle of memory against forget-
ting.") Historian Alan Riding notes that during the war
years that followed Maurice Gardette's murder, 75 percent of
French Jews were saved from deportation and death (despite
the longtime anti-Semitism of the French right wing), "ow-
ing to the courage of countless French men and women—
teachers, priests, nuns, resistance fighters, doctors, farmers,
and others."*

Inspired by this annual fall ritual of patriotic observance,
the historical memory of the eleventh pulses strong, its body's
blood a river of gratitude.

Nearby

RUE JEAN-PIERRE TIMBAUD   *The street is named for another*
Résistant *shot at Châteaubriant. Jean-Pierre Timbaud, the secretary of the steelworkers' union and a strike organizer during
the 1930s, faced the firing squad singing the "Marseillaise."* **La
Maison des Metallos** *(number 94), a community center with a
café, studios, and space for workers in the metal trades, is at
Esplanade Roger-Linet—the triangle formed by rue Jean-Pierre*

---

*Ian Buruma, review of Alan Riding, *And the Show Went On: Cultural Life in
Nazi-Occupied Paris*, in *The New York Review of Books*.

Timbaud, rue des Trois-Couronnes, and rue Morand, where there's also a mosque, children playing under the catalpa trees, and a version of Rodin's Thinker.

LES BELLES MIETTES *96, rue Jean-Pierre Timbaud. A quiet attractive bistro just next door to La Maison des Metallos.*

LE CANNIBALE *93, rue Jean-Pierre Timbaud; métro Belleville, Couronnes. An art deco café, with music. A nice place to celebrate* La Fête de la Musique *on Midsummer Night.*

L'AUTRE CAFÉ *62, rue Jean-Pierre Timbaud and rue Edouard Lockroy; métro, Parmentier, Oberkampf; www.lautrecafé.com. A low-key simpatico café-restaurant, with good food—especially the entrecôte grillée—and dining rooms on two floors. Exhibitions of local photography, sculpture, painting.*

ASTIER *44, rue Jean-Pierre Timbaud. www.bestrestaurants paris.com, with one of "the best cheese trays in the city" (Mark Bittman). Open seven nights a week.*

BOULEVARD RICHARD-LENOIR *From Bastille to République, this is a long tree-lined walk, the scene of food and clothing markets every Tues, Thurs, and Fri, 7–2.*

CANAL SAINT-MARTIN *Follow boulevard Richard-Lenoir and the tree-lined canal walk straight to* Square Jules-Ferry, *by turns idyllic and scruffy, never synthetic. The canal has nine locks, two swing bridges, and several arched footbridges. To the right, avenue Richerand leads to* l'Hôpital Saint-Louis, *the seventeenth-century public hospital for plague victims built by order of Henri IV, its inner red brick and stone quadrangle and garden courtyard the twin of* Place des Vosges, *a quiet retreat on a weekday morning.*

Square de la Roquette

SQUARE DE LA ROQUETTE

ENTRANCES: 147, rue de la Roquette; rue Servan; rue
   Merlan
MÉTRO: Père-Lachaise; Voltaire; Philippe Auguste
HOURS: daily, 7–dusk, according to the season

Walking up to *Roquette* from nearby *Maurice-Gardette,* or, better, from the other side of the city, from *Square du Vert Galant,* say, in the first *arrondissement,* or, best, from Passy in the sixteenth, you experience Paris in a way that only walking makes possible. "Walkers are practitioners of the city," as one theorist puts it: the "city is a language . . . and walking is the act of speaking that language." Only by using one's leg power to see one *arrondissement* after another can you get inside that language. Moving on foot from central or western Paris into the northeast enables the physical and emotional reverberations of "psychogeography," the sense of "the sudden change of ambience in a street within the space of a few meters, the evident division of the city into zones of distinct psychic atmospheres."* As you walk, it becomes obvious: the City of Light speaks many languages.

Since the revolution of 1968 (euphemistically referred to as *les événements,* or "the events" of 1968) this old area of insurrection—the plebeian northeast of the eleventh, twelfth, nineteenth, and twentieth *arrondissements,* which did not take much part in 1968—has been reconstituted. After years of

---

*Rebecca Solnit, "Paris, or Botanizing on the Asphalt," in *Wanderlust*: *A History of Walking.*

demolition and gentrification under former president Georges Pompidou (1969–1974), the mixed population has returned. In the streets around *rue de la Roquette,* the Paris proletariat has reestablished itself, marked by the return of immigrants, working families, artists, and "an intellectual but nonuniversity youth."*

Square de la Roquette mirrors the neighborhood, especially in the well-designed children's playground. The interplay of cultures among the kids, their parents, and caregivers make for delightful people-watching and eavesdropping. Above the playground—Roquette is built on a kind of *butte*—are winding paths, bench-lined of course, skirting flower beds that are glorious in spring: hyacinth, pansies, daisies, snowdrops, wildflowers, tulips all bloom beneath magnolias, palm trees, and eucalyptus. Never would you imagine the sinister history of these few acres as you sit enjoying the exuberance of the children at your back, the boys playing soccer below in the basketball court, the serenity of the people reading and talking on the benches.

At the square's entrance, there's a "History of Paris" plaque at the windows of the still-standing guardhouse. After its convent of nuns was closed after 1789, Roquette became for centuries a site of incarceration: of women, of incorrigible children ages six to twenty, and finally of four thousand *Résistantes* during the Occupation. The men's prison for murderers and death-row inmates was across *rue de la Roquette* in *rue de la Croix Faubin,* where the guillotine— "that shameful machine of human butchery," in the words of Louise Michel—operated until it was demolished in 1974.

Just inside the entrance to *Roquette* you face a high cas-

* Eric Hazan, "Red Paris," in *The Invention of Paris: A History in Footsteps.*

cading fountain that waters the palm trees and the flower gardens. Local people—there are few strangers here—sit in the companionable shade. Like so many calm green sanctuaries in Paris, this landscape bears a legacy of pain and injustice from the old world; stories of suffering are part of its buried landscape. But *Roquette* has been made over and made new in the image of a more generous and more fertile polity, a kind of urban oasis of comfort replacing an architecture of tyranny, prisons that looked like towering grim castles.

Nearby

RESTAURANT LA BOULANGERIE   *15, rue des Panoyaux; métro, Ménilmontant, a bit to the east, along boulevard Ménilmontant, heading away from rue de Ménilmontant. Information: 01.43.58.45.45. Open every day except Saturday lunch, Sunday, and Monday. Excellent food in a lovely first-floor interior, with an upstairs dining room. At the top of a narrow lane on a square resembling a movie set of old Paris.*

ÉGLISE NOTRE-DAME DE LA CROIX   *3, place de Ménilmontant, on Square Maurice Chevalier, at the head of rue Étienne Dolet, with stunning wooden sculptures of Christian icons by Joseph Pyrz. Kids kick a soccer ball atop the high front steps with a view, a setting in Brian De Palma's* Femme Fatale. *The sound of the church bells—"Christian beauty"*—fills the surrounding streets.*

LE MONTE-EN-L'AIR   *2, rue de la Mare, just behind the church. A good book-and-music store, an art gallery, and a terrace with chairs.*

---

*Leon Wieseltier, "Ring the Bells," *The New Republic.*

BISTRO MELAC   *42, rue Leon Frot (the extension of rue Saint-Maur, beyond Roquette); métro, Charonne. Closed Sundays and August. A first-rate family-run, friendly bistro, serving the famous and much-loved red meat from the Auvergne and, on Thursdays, the "Mac Melac," a burger-like sandwich with melted cantal on good bread. A relief statue,* Bacchus of Charonne, *is set into the wall above the entrance, and in the windows are quotes from satisfied writers.*

Parc des Buttes-Chaumont

PARC DES BUTTES-CHAUMONT

ENTRANCES: rue Manin; rue Botzaris
MÉTRO: Botzaris; Buttes-Chaumont
HOURS: daily, 7–dusk, according to the season

Monsieur Alphand had his work cut out for him when Haussmann and Napoleon III directed him to transform the foul terrain in eastern Paris into a scenic garden that would become *Buttes-Chaumont.* And once again the genius landscape engineer/architect pulled off an inspired metamorphosis. Today *Buttes-Chaumont* is one of the city's most popular parks, where sprawling and picnicking on the grass is permitted to weekending crowds from all over the city. Some visitors are aware that in an earlier life the park served as a quarry for gypsum—plaster of Paris—as well as a garbage dump. But its function in preceding centuries is less widely known. Historian Colin Jones evokes the long-ago horror of the countryside around what is now *Buttes-Chaumont:* in the Middle Ages, as far to the west as *Place du Colonel-Fabien,* this land was the site of the *gibbet of Montfaucon:*

Established by Saint Louis (1223–70) as a sign of royal justice over the city, . . . the gibbet was . . . an elaborate stone structure with some 16 columns, each ten meters high. From it literally scores of decaying criminals' bodies could be hanging at any time. The gibbet was a place of execution in its own right, but also the place of exhibition of the remains of individuals tortured and executed in one of the

many execution sites in Paris. . . . Bodies could be left
there for two or three years or more, at the end of which time,
crows and (in bad times) wolves having done their worst—
they were a gruesome sight, and their noisome stench wafted
towards the Faubourg du Temple. . . . In its garbage dump
years, this landscape also fed a plump army of rats, who
could strip a corpse to its skeleton within 24 hours.*

These days ***Buttes-Chaumont*** is considered a "legendary paradise," as poet Louis Aragon put it, "a vast expanse of kitschy pleasures"—Colin Jones again—a "romantic" and "fairy-tale-like park," in various guidebooks. Wandering the three miles of walking paths, up and down the gentle hills beneath the cedars of Lebanon, past a grotto with a waterfall, you'll come to a lake with a huge rock above it, which in turn is topped by a mock Corinthian temple: there are good views of *Montmartre* and *Saint-Denis* from up here. You can cross the lake on a suspension bridge or on the ***Pont des Suicides.*** There's also a children's carousel, a few cafés and the popular ***Rosa Bonheur restaurant/ginguette,*** open for dancing, eating, and drinking (Wed–Sun until midnight), even when the park is closed. ***Rosa Bonheur*** (1822–1899) was the most famous female French painter of the nineteenth century (*The Horse Fair* hangs in the Metropolitan Museum of Art in New York City), scorned in her day for wearing pants, smoking cigarettes, and enjoying the company of women.

Many tourists do not make it out this far from the city center, but the robust and exuberant Julia Child (with her husband, Paul) found her way, on foot, early in her time as a Parisian:

---

* Colin Jones, *Paris, The Biography of a City.*

> *Paris was wonderfully walkable. . . . one could easily hike*
> *from the Place de la Concorde to the top of Montmartre in*
> *a half-hour. . . . One cold afternoon just before New Year's,*
> *Paul and I strolled up to the Buttes-Chaumont park. At*
> *the top of the hill, by the little Greek temple, we looked back*
> *at Sacré-Coeur on Montmartre, now silhouetted through*
> *layers of mist by the declining sun. . . .* *

Then they retired to a nearby cozy bistro, complete with cats, dogs, neighborhood characters, and two monkeys squealing and chattering.

In the streets bordering the park today, there are a number of ethnic bistros and cafés, including *L'Éstampe* at 74, rue de Botzaris. In the picturesque *Mouzaïa District* (named for a place in Algeria)—between *Buttes-Chaumont* and *Square de la Butte-du-Chapeau-Rouge*—in the streets around *rue Miguel-Hidalgo* and *rue de Mouzaïa,* you can imitate the indefatigable Julia, who loved to "intentionally wander off the beaten path" all over the city and no doubt discovered these pedestrian cobbled streets of terraced villas and small gardens of fruit trees and flowers, perhaps en route to the *Danube* métro.

Nearby

PARC DE LA VILLETTE   *North of Buttes-Chaumont; métro, Porte de Pantin near the avenue Jean-Jaurès southern entrance, with its good Information center to help you get the lay of Villette's vast lawns and many buildings. The park goes on and on for miles, past one innovative themed garden after another—the Garden of Mirrors, of Dunes, of Winds, of Shadows, of Dragons (with a*

---

* Julia Child, *My Life in France.*

dragon slide), all joined together by the Promenade des Jardins. Other highlights (near the southern entrance) include the Conservatoire de Paris*; the* Musée de la Musique*, with five floors of instruments, an overview of the history of Western music, and special exhibits— Chopin's bicentennial tribute in 2010 was superb; the* **Café de la Musique;** *and the* **Cité de la Musique** *auditorium, featuring great concerts and performers (www.cite-musique.fr). The huge Cité des Sciences et de l'Industrie, like a number of the other buildings, rises above abandoned abattoirs: La Villette was originally the site of the city's main slaughterhouse.*

PARC DE BELLEVILLE   *Métro, Belleville. Walk from* **boulevard de Belleville,** *the bustling, gritty hub of artists, students, and immigrant residents from the Middle East, Africa, and Asia, up the hill of* **rue de Belleville** *(no 72 is the legendary birthplace of* **Edith Piaf***), turn right into* **rue Piaf***, and keep climbing, bearing right at the top toward the park's welcoming panorama, a higher overview of Paris than from Montmartre. Descending the steep paths and steps, beneath arches of wisteria, you'll come into the lower park meadow, unforgettable in June when the roses are in bloom, the neighborhood children run free, and people relax on the grass. The streets around the park give a sense of a contemporary Paris not to be had elsewhere: the ateliers, squats, and exhibits of artists in* **rue Ramponeau***; the studios and work spaces in **rue des Couronnes,** with access to the rose gardens. Further downhill is the* **Couronnes** *métro.*

Père-Lachaise Cemetery

PÈRE-LACHAISE

ENTRANCES: boulevard de Ménilmontant (maps of the
    cemetery are for sale); avenue du Père-Lachaise; rue
    de la Roquette; rue de la Réunion
MÉTRO: Père-Lachaise; Gambetta; Philippe Auguste
HOURS: Easter–Sept, 8–6; Oct–Easter, 8–dusk

Colette (1873–1954), ecstatic lover of nature, would approve mightily of her final resting place. There are twelve thousand trees in *Père-Lachaise Cemetery,* avenues of cypresses, sycamores, tall, ancient chestnuts, a thick sheltering green roof over the cemetery's 105 acres of unspoiled beauty. Flowers are planted around the graves, some garlanding the monuments, symbolizing perpetual affection for the dead. "Throughout my existence," Colette wrote not long before she died, "I have studied flowering more than any other manifestation of life. It is there, for me, that the essential drama resides, and not in death, which is just a banal defeat."*

Among the 300,000 men and women buried in Paris's largest cemetery are icons of a prodigious flowering of French civilization who inspired a cultural reverence for that flowering in science, philosophy, politics, and especially the arts—the writers, painters, sculptors, singers, composers, and cinéastes who make us love life more. Time spent in *Père-Lachaise* quickens that love. There's no hurry here, no distractions. You can stroll the silent hillsides, follow the long,

---

*Colette, "The Ripening Seed," quoted in Judith Thurman, *Secrets of the Flesh: A Life of Colette.*

winding cobbled paths, stirred to your depths as you suddenly come upon the graves of Proust and Wilde, Delescluze, Daumier, and Poulenc. You can stop midway at a bench along a steep avenue to contemplate this landscape of memory. Memory, said Gertrude Stein: the only true immortality. (Her grave is at the eastern edge of *avenue Circulaire*.)

From the heights of *Père-Lachaise,* you see on your map that Chopin lies down the hill, near the center, not far from Colette, or from another of George Sand's lovers, Alfred de Musset. Delacroix (under black lava) is to the west, his artistic style—a striving for a surprising violent exotic beauty*— the romantic painter's version of his beloved Chopin's romantic music. Balzac, another friend of Delacroix, and another genius of that great nineteenth-century artistic explosion, rests in the same section. Again in the vicinity of Colette's flower-strewn black granite are the lovers Héloise (1101–1164) and Abélard (1079–1142), together in death, in eternal defiance of the ecclesiastical powers that forced them apart in life. Their bodies were moved into *Père-Lachaise*—along with Molière and La Fontaine—in an effort to attract the important dead to what was a remote section of Paris when the cemetery was opened by Napoleon in 1804. In the seventeenth century the land had belonged to the Jesuits, who called it *Mont Louis*; the prominent Jesuit François de la Chaise d'Aix, confessor to Louis XIV, lived here and retired to a splendid country house on Mont Louis. Supposedly, the simpatico confessor and the young king-to-be watched the civil revolt called the Fronde (1649–1652) from here ("the hill of Charonne"), that traumatic vigil the source of the Sun King's lifelong fear and hatred of the mob (the *frondeurs*), which would

---

* Umberto Eco, ed. *History of Beauty*.

eventually drive him to abandon Paris and move the royal court to Versailles.

The cemetery's associations with—and proximity to—political violence did not disappear in *le grande siècle*. Two hundred years later, the Paris Communards, in rebellion against the remnant Versailles government of Napoleon III's autocratic regime, made their last stand here among the tombstones (and in the nearby streets of Ménilmontant, Charonne, and Belleville). Finally subdued on May 28, 1871, 147 rebels were rounded up and shot against the eastern perimeter wall; the corpses of another thousand Communards were dumped in pits against the same wall. Today the *Mur des Fédérés*—the Wall of the Communards—to the right and down a few steps off *avenue Circulaire*—is a site of annual pilgrimage to commemorate the bravery of the working classes and the savagery of a government terrified of popular revolt.* Now classified as a national historical monument, the Wall is always decorated with the flowers and wreaths left by pilgrims who arrive in all seasons. (The autumn foliage is beautiful here.)

In the same corner of the cemetery, opposite the Wall, are the memorials to the murdered Résistants and the victims of the deportations to the Nazi labor and death camps in World War II. Buried close to the Résistants is *Edith Piaf* (1915–1963), native of Belleville, where she grew up homeless and starving until her voice reached her natural audience, the ordinary workers and marginalized poor of Paris. Hers is the most visited grave in this *campo santo*.

The Dutch filmmaker Heddy Honigmann's documentary *Forever* unfolds an elegiac profile of the consoling beauty of *Père-Lachaise*. Some last words of Colette's resonate with

---

* Colin Jones, *Paris: The Biography of a City.*

the film's muted joy: "What a wonderful life I've had. I only wish I'd realized it sooner."

Nearby

JARDIN NATUREL   *At 120, rue de la Réunion and a few steps from the Réunion exit from the cemetery; métro, Alexandre Dumas; open 7:30–5:30. The city created this nature reserve as an educational resource for neighborhood schoolchildren who study the ecosystem here. There are woods, a pond with water lilies, fish, dragonflies, frogs, all sorts of insects. With two hundred varieties of plants and singing birds fluttering through woods dense with laurel and spirea, this is a man-made haven for nature lovers and people watchers.*

LIBRAIRIE EQUIPAGES   *61, rue de Bagnolet. To the right from rue de la Réunion, a smallish but good bookstore with helpful service.*

LE MERLE MOQUEUR   *51, rue de Bagnolet. A large bookstore with a strong children's section that hosts readings and discussion groups; information: www.lemerlemocquer.fr. Rue de Bagnolet and the streets between it and the cemetery have a warm, small-town intimacy.*

CEMETERY OF ÉGLISE SAINT-GERMAIN DE CHARONNE   *111, rue de Bagnolet (on Place Saint-Blaise); métro, Gambetta. From place Gambetta walk down rue Stendhal and descend the staircase alongside pretty houses; from the square in front of the church (fifteenth century, though the first church on this site dates from the ninth), you will see the entrance to the cemetery, a bucolic sanctuary on a hill of cherry trees in April as well as flowering shrubbery. You're in the ancient village of Charonne, still a countryside-within-the-city. From the cemetery, bear left onto rue de Bagnolet and continue to* **Jardin Debrousse,** *148, rue de Bagnolet, a sprawling riot of bright flowers and schoolchildren on weekday afternoons. These are the remaining grounds of the Château de Bagnolet estate, originally twice the size of Père-Lachaise. Farther along rue de Bagnolet is métro Porte de Bagnolet.*

SOURCES

The dates of publication refer to the year of the editions the author has read, consulted, or cited in writing this book.

Austrian, Delia. *Juliette Récamier*, 1922.

Babelon, Jean-Pierre. "Henri IV, urbaniste de Paris," in *Festival du Marais*, 1966.

Balzac, Honoré de. *Cousin Bette*, 2002.

Bazoches, Guy de. "Description de Paris vers 1175," *Chronicles & Letters*, 1961.

Benjamin, Walter. *The Arcades Project*, 1997.

Brooks, Peter. *Henry James Goes to Paris*, 2007.

Brown, Frederick. *For the Soul of France: Culture Wars in the Age of Dreyfus*, 2010.

Butler, Ruth. *Rodin: The Shape of Genius*, 1993.

Cahill, Thomas. *Pope John XXIII*, 2002.

Camus, Albert. *Notebooks 1942–1951*, 1963.

Caro, Ina. *Paris to the Past*, 2011.

Child, Julia. *My Life in France*, 2007.

Clark, T. J. *The Painting of Modern Life: Paris in the Art of Manet and His Followers*, 1984.

Cobb, Richard. *Paris and Elsewhere*, ed. David Gilmour, 1998.

Colette. *Claudine in Paris*, 2001.

———. *Places*, 1971.

———. *The Ripening Seed*, 1925.

Collins, Larry, and Dominique Lapierre. *Is Paris Burning?* 1991.

Dallas, Gregor. *Métro Stop Paris*, 2008.

Delacroix, Eugène. *The Journal of Eugène Delacroix*, ed. Hubert Wellington, 2004.

Duras, Marguerite. *The War (Le Douleur)*, 1986.

Eco, Umberto, ed. *History of Beauty*, 2010.

Eisler, Benita. *Chopin's Funeral*, 2003.

Flaubert, Gustave. "The Legend of Saint Julien," *Three Tales*, 1999.

Furst, Alan. *Red Gold*, 1999.

Gray, Francine du Plessix. *At Home with the Marquis de Sade: A Life*, 1999.

———. *Madame De Staël: The First Modern Woman*, 2008.

———. "Mother Love: Madame de Sévigne," *Adam and Eve in the City: Selected Nonfiction*, 1987.

———. *Rage and Fire: A Life of Louise Colet—Pioneer Feminist, Literary Star, Flaubert's Muse*, 1994.

Halter, Clara, and Jean-Michel Wilmotte, *Peace Wall*. www.murpour lapaix.org.

Harlan, Elizabeth. *George Sand*, 2004.

Hazan, Eric. *The Invention of Paris: A History in Footsteps*, 2010.

Hemingway, Ernest. "The Snows of Kilimanjaro," 1936.

Horne, Alistair. *Seven Ages of Paris*, 2004.

———. *La Belle France: A Short History*, 2006.

Howett, Catherine, Charles A. Lewis, and S. Kaplan, "The Healing Power of Gardens," in *The Meaning of Gardens*, eds. Francis and Hester, 1992.

Huston, Nancy. *The Mark of the Angel*, 2000.

James, Henry. *The Ambassadors*, 1985.

Jones, Colin. *Paris: The Biography of a City*, 2004.

Judt, Tony. "Historian's Progress," *New York Review of Books*, March 11, 2010.

Knecht, Robert J. *The French Renaissance Court*, 2008.

Lafayette, Madame de. *The Princesse de Clèves*, 1992.

Lee, Hermione. *Edith Wharton*, 2007.

Littlewood, Ian. *Paris: A Literary Companion*, 1989.

Malraux, André. *Speech at the Panthéon, December 19, 1964;* Web citation: www.oocities.org/resistancehistory/malraux.

Maritain, Jacques. *France My Country*, 1941.

Marnham, Patrick. *Resistance and Betrayal: The Death and Life of the Greatest Hero of the French Resistance*, 2000.

Maurois, André. *A History of France*, 1948.

Mercier, Louis Sebastien. *Tableau de Paris*, 2010.

Mitford, Nancy. *Madame de Pompadour*, 1954.

Obelensky, Valerian. *Russians in Exile: The History of the Diaspora;* Web citation: valobel.blogspot.com./russians-in-exile.history.

Pearson, Hesketh. *Henry of Navarre: The King Who Dared*, 1963.

Pétrement, Simone. *Simone Weil: A Life*, 1976.

Powys, John Cowper. "Paul Verlaine," in *Suspended Judgments: Essays on Books and Sensations;* Web citation: www.gutenberg.org/ebooks.

Prose, Francine. Introduction to Honoré de Balzac, *Cousin Bette,* 2002.

Riding, Alan. *And the Show Went On: Cultural Life in Nazi-Occupied Paris,* 2010.

Rilke, Rainer Maria. *Letters on Life,* ed. Ulrich Baer, 2006.

Robb, Graham. *Parisians: An Adventure History of Paris,* 2010.

Rodin, Auguste. *Cathedrals of France,* 1965.

Roth, Joseph. *Report from a Parisian Paradise: Essays, 1925–1939.*

Rowlands, Penelope, ed. *Paris Was Ours,* 2011.

Saint-Exupéry, Antoine de. *Wartime Writings 1939–1944,* 1986.

Schiff, Stacy. *Saint-Exupéry: A Biography,* 2006.

———. *The Great Improvisation: Franklin, France, and The Birth of America,* 2005.

Schurmann, Michael. *Paris Movie Walks,* 2009.

Sciolino, Elaine. "Hidden Gardens of Paris," *New York Times,* June 29, 2008.

Sévigné, Madame de. *Letters,* ed. Leonard Tancock, 1982.

Solnit, Rebecca. *Wanderlust: A History of Walking,* 2000.

Springsted, Eric O., ed. *Simone Weil,* 1998.

Temko, Allan. *Notre-Dame of Paris,* 1962.

Thurman, Judith. *Secrets of the Flesh: A Life of Colette,* 1999.

Weber, Caroline. "Yvon's Paris," *New York Times Book Review,* December 3, 2010.

Wieseltier, Leon. "Ring the Bells," *The New Republic,* April 23, 2008.

ACKNOWLEDGMENTS

My thanks, as always, to my husband, Tom Cahill, still the best and most fun fellow traveler since we first stopped in Paris on our long-ago honeymoon summer, sating ourselves in the old *Les Halles* at 4 AM, promising we'd come back. We have, regularly, happily, to visit our son Joseph, filmmaker and artist, whose help with this book about his new home city has been good-humored and patient.

I thank my friends in Paris for welcoming me, visit upon visit, guiding me to the off-the-beaten-track Paris known only to natives: Suzanne Ranoux, an inimitable and savvy companion of good cheer who introduced me to so many places, restaurants, the hotel Lutetia, cafés, concerts in Saint-Sulpice, exhibits at *le Grand Palais*, and the rose festival in the Bagatelle. Camille Dalsace welcomed me so often to her *crèperie* in *l'onzième*, most memorably to celebrate the annual and magical *Fête de la Musique*. Anne Laure Jardry and Renaud Guerrero led me up and down the charming streets of their home turf, *la Butte-aux-Cailles*, and those surrounding Parc Montsouris. I will never forget the *esprit* of the artists of *La Forge* in Belleville and especially the hospitality of French rocker Arthur H (*"L'Homme du Monde"*) at his spectacular performance at the Olympia. Monsieur Didier of Hotel Beaumarchais remains a warm and efficient *hôtelier*. And all my visits to Paris begin and end inside the Village Voice bookshop on *rue Princesse*, where Odile Hellier, legendary bookseller, has put into my hands some of the best sources I have used to understand and cherish her city's culture of memory.

I would like to thank everyone at St. Martin's Press in New York, especially my editor, Charles Spicer, whose expertise, warmth, and enthusiasm for our project made the work of it a pleasure. Thanks, too, to his assistants, Yaniv Soha and April Osborn, as well as to the book's designer, Fritz Metsch, and to Rob Grom for the beautiful cover.

I would also like to thank publisher Matthew Shear, managing editor Amelie Littell, production manager Adriana Coada, production editor Geraldine Van Dusen, and all the professionals behind the scenes who day-in and day-out continue to make book publishing a creative adventure.

My thanks, finally, to my agent, John F. Thornton. And above all, I am grateful to photographer Marion Ranoux for the beauty of her images and the unfailing graciousness of her collaboration.

INDEX

Italic page numbers indicate photographs.

ABOUT THE AUTHOR

SUSAN CAHILL, PH.D., has published four other travel books, *Desiring Italy: Women Writers Celebrate a Country and a Culture; The Smiles of Rome; For the Love of Ireland;* and, with her husband, Thomas Cahill, *A Literary Guide to Ireland.* She is the editor of the bestselling Women and Fiction series and author of the novel *Earth Angels.* She lives in New York City and spends a few months in Paris every year.

ABOUT THE PHOTOGRAPHER

MARION RANOUX, an experienced freelance photographer and translator into French of Czech literature, is a lifelong resident of Paris and connoisseur of the hidden places of her native city.